THE
FI5TH
GOSPEL

THE FI5TH GOSPEL

BOBBY CONWAY
WITH JEFF KINLEY

HARVEST HOUSE PUBLISHERS
EUGENE, OREGON

Cover design by Harvest House Publishers, Inc., Eugene, Oregon

Published in association with William K. Jensen Literary Agency, 119 Bampton Court, Eugene, Oregon 97404

THE FIFTH GOSPEL
Copyright © 2014 by Bobby Conway
Published by Harvest House Publishers
Eugene, Oregon 97402
www.harvesthousepublishers.com

ISBN 978-0-7369-5845-5

Library of Congress Cataloging-in-Publication Data
    Conway, Bobby, 1973-
    The fifth gospel / Bobby Conway, with Jeff Kinley.
       pages cm
    ISBN 978-0-7369-5845-5 (pbk.)
    ISBN 978-0-7369-5846-2 (eBook)
    1. Christian life. 2. Witness bearing (Christianity) I. Title.
    BV4501.3.C6627 2014
    248.4—dc23

2013043555

Printed in the United States of America

14 15 16 17 18 19 20 21 22 23 / VP-JH / 10 9 8 7 6 5 4 3 2 1

To my beloved wife and children:
Heather, Haley, and Dawson.
May being a Fifth-Gospel Christian
never cease being our family ideal.

Acknowledgments

Thanks to…

Jeff Kinley for your masterful help and contribution to this book.

Bill Jensen for being such a great literary agent and champion of the *Fifth Gospel* concept.

Harvest House Publishers for taking on this project.

LaRae Weikert for believing in this book.

Rod Morris for your insights and editorial help.

The late Gypsy Smith, whose quote inspired me to write *The Fifth Gospel*.

Life Fellowship Church, staff, leaders, and fellow elders for your prayers, support, and love.

The Lord Jesus Christ—for apart from You, I can do nothing.

CONTENTS

RELEASING THE LOST GOSPEL

*"The gospel is not a doctrine of the tongue, but of life. It
cannot be grasped by reason and memory only, but
it is fully understood when it possesses the whole soul
and penetrates to the inner recesses of the heart."*

JOHN CALVIN

Every so often somebody strings together a set of words that
have transforming power. Words that serve as a launchpad,
providing the opportunity for cultural transformation. Words that
carry shaping influence. Such is the case with a quote attributed
to Rodney (Gypsy) Smith, a nineteenth-century British evangelist who passionately led evangelistic campaigns to countries such
as Australia, South Africa, and the United States. On one occasion
he quipped, "There are five Gospels: Matthew, Mark, Luke, John,
and the Christian, but most people never read the first four." Talk
about Twitter material. Little did Gypsy Smith realize his words
would be turned into a book someday! These are not mere words.
They are words with a challenge. A challenge to be something. In
this case, *a living Gospel*!

The early church grasped the gravity of Gypsy Smith's words by
living the Gospel. It was the Gospel fleshed out in their daily lives

that made the Gospel so compelling to those getting saved. They lived as if they *really* believed it. With conviction, fervor, zeal, and a white-hot passion for Jesus Christ. Their belief was tangible. So real, so firm, so raw was their conviction that their message blasted off through their lives from Jerusalem and would eventually reach out to the ends of the earth. Unfortunately, today, many Christians treat the Gospel like fine china, brought out only on special occasions. Or like an ancient artifact displayed in a glass case, something you talk about in the event someone inquires about it. The only "lost Gospel" is the one housed in the hearts of believers, a Gospel pleading to be released.

> This book is an invitation to go beyond merely reading the Gospels to actually living the Gospels.

This book is an invitation to go beyond merely reading the Gospels to actually living the Gospels. To visibly display the Good News of salvation through the Messiah and Redeemer of humankind. *The Fifth Gospel* is "another" Gospel, *not in addition* to the four found in Scripture, but instead a living incarnation of them. Not an inspired Gospel, but an inspiring one. This was Jesus' original intention, for ordinary people like us to live *inspiring* lives, pointing others to the only message, the only *Person*, who can give them hope for not only this life but also the next.

The Gospel of Jesus is simply beautiful. Period. There's nothing like it on earth in depth or scope. It has no equal in power. The riches it holds are immeasurable. It interacts with the worst part of humanity, yet remains pure. It can still be found today in its glorious form, without unnecessary extras added to it to enhance its market appeal. No, *this* Gospel is legit all by itself, understood simply and plainly from the lips of Jesus or the pages of His Bible. But therein lies a problem—actually two dilemmas.

The first is that many people in our culture rarely seek truth by opening a Bible. Sad but true. In a world of growing hostility toward the church and evangelicalism, it may be wishful thinking that this generation's eyes ever fall on the words of Matthew, Mark, Luke, or John.

But the second obstacle in displaying this beautiful Gospel is that, from the very beginning, Jesus intended His truth and character to be revealed, not only through the printed page, but also through the *lives* of His followers. It's this largely unknown, *incarnated* Gospel that our world knows so little about.

The Fifth Gospel is an appeal for a watching world to witness the reality of Christ through the lives of His followers.

Of course, such a task presents an inherent challenge. It's risky. Transparent. Possibly awkward. A little more authentic than we're used to. Even potentially dangerous. But considering that the majority of our unbelieving friends will likely never read the first four Gospels, shouldn't we at least give them the opportunity to read the fifth one? Isn't it time for us to *become* a visible witness for the One we profess to love so much?

> Isn't it time for us to *become* a visible witness for the One we profess to love so much?

"Sharing the Gospel" spans the spectrum within the Christian community. On one end are the morality police—those Gospel grenade-launching believers who see it as their mission to expose and condemn every ill of culture, further alienating non-Christians from anything remotely connected to Jesus. Perceived hate typically produces hate in return. And as a result, we're often viewed as the playground bully, the villain of the story. Tragic.

On the other end of this spectrum are those believers who feel obliged to make restitution for two thousand years of mistakes made by Christians and their church, to right the wrongs done in the name of Christ—the Crusades, the Inquisition, the Salem Witch Trials, abuse, moral failure, and the slick, modern, market-savvy methods of the megachurch movement. It doesn't take a scholar or historian to understand that in both ancient and modern times, Christians haven't always gotten it right.

You could fill a book—a library of books—with the ways Christians have *missed the mark*, to use a biblical expression. There's no shortage of power-hungry pastors and ecclesiastical Pharisees in our day. But neither is the cause of the Gospel helped by the explosion of young bloggers with just enough knowledge of history to be dangerous and almost no understanding of Scripture or how to interpret it. Their mantra: "If we're just nice to people, they'll see our perspective. Don't judge anyone's beliefs. And whatever you do, don't offend *anybody!*" Their apparent goal is for all humanity to coexist as one, singing in three-part harmony some sort of postmillennial world peace anthem. They believe if we simply say we're sorry, tone down our language, and redefine some key biblical truths to accommodate our culture's tolerance-based morality, that'll do it.

But will it?

What this naïve perspective fails to take into account is the basic animosity unbelievers have for God and all things biblical.[1] There is a sin nature and there is a devil. While their motives may be commendable, redefining truth and Scripture will be as effective in changing the world as shooting a squirt gun at a forest fire. Meanwhile, the Bible-club-wielding Christians are tossing gasoline on that same fire.

We Christians are a mess, aren't we?

Many of today's Christ followers are either ridden with guilt for not preaching the Gospel or so silent about it that no one really knows they're a Christian. And the vast majority of us don't have a clue about communicating our faith and translating it through a lifestyle that actually makes sense to the average person.

This book will help you do that.

It will help you wrestle with some of the critical issues involved in living out your faith in front of a watching, and sometimes

> This book will help you wrestle with some of the critical issues involved in living out your faith in front of a watching world.

not-so-friendly world. It's not a book of recipes but a manual of life skills. But before we construct this life apologetic together, we first have to do some *de*-construction. We have to go *back* before we go forward. We have to reject the notion that the louder the gospel music, the more powerful it becomes and that if we just turn up the volume, people will listen. Similarly, we also have to stop cowering behind a twisted tolerance and blending our values with the world's. If there's nothing distinctive about our faith, then we have little to offer our friends. Jesus called us the "light of the world." Our mission is to neither dim that light nor to blind people with it.

This book is not an apology to our culture, with chapter upon chapter exposing Christianity's faults and failures. Rather, it's an *apologetic*. The difference? One says, "I'm sorry" while the other says, "Here are believable, convincing reasons why Jesus Christ is real!"

So now, as we begin this journey and dig into the following chapters of this book, I hope to show you that one of the greatest convincers or *de*-convincers of Christianity is Christians. When the Christian lives like his Christ, he moves beyond the mere Gospel in print and begins to demonstrate the Gospel in action. In person.

> One of the greatest convincers or *de*-convincers of Christianity is Christians.

This is the passion of God's heart—to unleash His transforming Gospel through *you*! The question is, *are you ready?*

Chapter 1

WHAT THE WORLD NEEDS NOW IS...?

*"Where one man reads the Bible,
a hundred read you and me."*

D.L. Moody

Some experiences in life mark you forever. They are memories custom-made by God to remind you of His presence and powerful love. Like an internal scrapbook of unforgettable photographs, these life episodes define your story, contributing to God's masterpiece, giving your life here a sense of meaning.

Coffee from Heaven

One of those moments for me came one sunny morning in a local coffee shop. Call it a divine appointment or happy accident. For me, it's what can only be described as a God-thing. That's how I describe the moment I bumped into Trent.

Trent was a neighbor of mine. A likeable guy. Friendly. Intelligent. A good member of our community. There was only one problem.

Trent was gay.

And not just casual gay either. Trent lived in an openly homosexual relationship with his partner just down the street from our house. Most Christians today struggle with how to respond to gay people. We trend toward the extremes, pendulum-swinging from wide-open acceptance of virtually anything to ultra-legalistic, self-righteous rudeness. Thankfully, Trent's sexual orientation didn't deter me from being his friend or showing God's love to him. And so, that morning over a cup of dark roast, we struck up a conversation, and before long the topic turned to God. Though obviously disillusioned with the church, to my surprise Trent was nevertheless still hungry for truth and spirituality. You could see it in his eyes and hear it in his voice.

During our conversation I said something that struck a chord with Trent, opening up his heart a bit.

"Trent, unfortunately most churches want people like you to agree with them on every point before they will accept you. But I think we've got it backward. In fact, as I read my Bible, I see Jesus accepting those He had strong disagreements with."

Trent's eyes widened, as if a light had been turned on inside. And that's when he began sharing his story with me. He had grown up in a religious home where his parents were heavy on legalism and light on grace. That, combined with repeated abuse, understandably caused Trent to become disillusioned, confused, and disconnected from anything (and anyone) connected to God.

My heart broke for Trent. Though I differed with him morally, I still accepted him relationally. God's love and compassion guided our random meeting that day, and to my surprise, not long afterward Trent and his partner invited my family over for dinner one night. Some Christians may have trouble imagining a pastor and his

> Trent's sexual orientation didn't deter me from being his friend or showing God's love to him.

> Unbelievers do watch us, secretly wondering if what we have is real or just religious pretense.

family having dinner with a homosexual couple, but last time I checked, God still loves people, so we gladly accepted the invitation.

Following that evening, I'd run into Trent from time to time, and one day, he stopped by my house and said, "Bobby, you probably don't know this, but I've been watching you. I see you outside playing with your kids. I see the way you relate to them." My first thought was, *Oops, I hope he's seen me on my good days*. Nevertheless, I was reminded that unbelievers do watch us, secretly wondering if what we have is real or just religious pretense.

Then one morning Trent knocked on my door to tell me he and his partner were reading the book of John together. I almost choked on my coffee! He said that God was working in his life. Shortly afterward, Trent showed up again to tell us he had finally fallen in love with Jesus Christ. In fact, God became so real to him that he broke off his relationship with his partner and moved out. His passion for Christ continued to grow, and in time he met and married a wonderful woman.

It had been a few years since I had seen Trent, and I often wondered how he was doing. Then one day a few months ago I was eating lunch at a local steakhouse, and to my surprise in walked Trent with his wife and their little child. It's hard to describe the feelings of satisfaction that overwhelmed me. Even as I write this, I'm still moved.

Trent's story reminds me of Jesus' words, "Those who are well have no need of a physician, but those who are sick."[1] We often forget that Christianity is not a philosophy to be argued but a Person to be known. To be sure, our values stand in stark contrast to many in our culture. Finding areas of disagreement really isn't much of a challenge, is it? The real challenge is to build bridges, not walls.

Looking back, all Trent really needed to get on the road toward

> We often forget that Christianity is not a philosophy to be argued but a Person to be known.

life change was for an ordinary Christian to accept him as a human being, as someone God loves and for whom Christ died. Today I clearly see the reflection of Jesus in Trent. That experience taught me that no one is too difficult or too far gone for God to reach.

Starting from Square One

If we're to effectively represent Jesus to our world, we must choose to trust God to change our minds and hearts about certain things. And that journey begins with honesty, authenticity, and answering some tough questions about our faith.

"Does the world really need Jesus?"

One of those questions defines us as believers. It's one that uncovers the foundation of our faith, revealing what it's really built upon. So here it is. Are you ready? That question is:

"Does the world really need Jesus? I mean c'mon…really?"

Some Christians may be offended by this question. Some may even protest. Others might wonder why we even need to ask it at all. But it's a fair question, and a critical one that touches the very heart of Christianity.

Do people need Jesus…or not?

Ours is a faith that unswervingly believes "God so loved the world, that he gave his only Son."[2] We believe the crux of Christianity is the cross, where God's eternal love and atoning sacrifice are displayed. At no other time in human history has God so plainly and blatantly revealed Himself than at Calvary. At no point has He so graphically uncovered His heart for mankind. It was there, on a hill outside Jerusalem, the Messiah bled for us, suffering hellish agony and sin-induced banishment, all the while enduring the brutal wrath of a holy and righteous God.

The exclamation point to this graphic love letter to us was the resurrection—Jesus' conquering moment of triumph over sin, Satan, and the grave. This is what Christians are all about, right? It's how we are saved. Take away the cross and we're no different from any other religious idea. It's Jesus Christ, His death and resurrection.

Strip away all the modern church fluff and this is what you find at the core of our faith.[3] It's essential. Nonnegotiable. Undeniable. It's what makes us who we are. It's what makes Christians "Christian." And it's why Jesus is the answer to all of life's deepest issues.

The only question is: Do we really believe it?

Of course you may nod your head in agreement, but how can you be sure, other than the fact that you think and believe it to be true?

It doesn't take a scientific study to prove there's a Grand Canyon-sized difference between what many Christians say they believe and how they actually live. And there are those who are more than willing to point that out. But imagine how things would be different if our lives mirrored what we say we "believe with all our heart." Would we be more like the Christ we claim to follow? After all, the word *Christian* means "Christ follower." But how many professing believers are thoroughly convinced that without Christ, our families, friends, classmates, neighbors, and coworkers are incomplete and lost, destined for eternal wrath?

What about you? Are you convinced? And how would you know?

Some argue that believing Jesus is "the only way" may have worked okay in the first century, when people were still digging water wells by hand, using candles, and living in mud huts. But how does faith in an unseen, supernatural Savior hold up in an age of science, reason, and technological wonders? Is this ancient Christian belief of ours still plausible? Is it reasonable? Does it work for the twenty-first century?

> How does faith in an unseen, supernatural Savior hold up in an age of science, reason, and technological wonders?

These are some of the critical issues we must explore together. For if they're true, they provide convincing credibility to all Christ's other claims. But if not, then everything we believe is negotiable and understandably suspect. And we, of all people, are to be pitied for believing in a very old, religious fairy tale.[4]

Holding on to this one core truth about Jesus can feel like riding a homemade raft in a Gulf Coast hurricane. Strong cultural winds and a constant moral crosscurrent toss the exclusivity of Jesus around to such a degree that it's become highly inappropriate to even believe it anymore. The religious correctness of our day has bullied Christ's Bride into silence, with some even conceding that the world will turn out just fine in the end—with or without a Jewish messiah.

> The religious correctness of our day has bullied Christ's Bride into silence.

But have you ever stopped to consider just why it's so hard for some people to believe in Jesus as the perfect path to forgiveness, happiness, fulfillment, and heaven?

Mini Gods or Many Gods?

We live in an age marked by "religious pluralism," which says no one religion (especially Christianity) holds the exclusive title to "absolute truth" (if there even is such a thing). Religious pluralism says all religions ultimately lead to one nebulous God, the Creator and Savior of us all. Tolerance, acceptance, and "personal belief" have become the new path to contentment, peace, and world unity.

While it is important for Christians to effectively and lovingly relate to a plurality of people and to be tolerant of others in that we are patient, kindhearted, and gentle, we are not to be tolerant as in passive or pluralistic in that we fail to stand for the exclusive truth claims of Christ.

Unfortunately, today, those who believe in a first-century Jewish Rabbi as "*the* way" are seen as harsh, mean-spirited, arrogant, and backward. And who wants to be like that? However, simply swap that definite article (*the*) for an *a* and instantly Jesus (and His followers) become a lot more palatable. One little word change and the Gospel aroma magically becomes more pleasant in an all-inclusive world. It reveals whether you're an exclusivist (a belief that only one religion is true) or a pluralist (all religions lead to God). Besides, it just sounds plain mean to exclude people, doesn't it? God wouldn't exclude people. God is love. He loves everybody the same, right?

And that's usually the point in the conversation where things start getting really uncomfortable and awkward. Raised in a secular climate of uber-tolerance, many Christians struggle to explain why kind, sincere, and devout followers of other faiths will miss heaven by a long shot. For example, how would you respond to a friend who challenged you with the following statements:

Many Christians struggle to explain why devout followers of other faiths will miss heaven by a long shot.

> "It doesn't matter what you believe as long as you're sincere."

> "As long as it works for you and makes you happy."

> "There is no such thing as ultimate (or absolute) truth."

> "I believe there are many ways to God."

> "It's rude to say one person's religion is better than another's."

> "It takes everyone's truth to equal the truth."

> "What makes you think your religion is right and everyone else is wrong?"

Any of these sound familiar? It is now socially unacceptable to criticize another person's religious beliefs (unless, of course, you're slamming Christianity). But keep in mind that, historically, ours has always been a creedal faith, meaning our beliefs direct and influence our attitudes and actions. Since its inception, Christianity has made a bold claim concerning the identity of the one true God and His Son Jesus. And that belief has enjoyed a relatively trouble-free existence in countries and cultures governed or influenced by Judeo-Christian beliefs. But not so today, where this foundational truth has taken a beating in the marketplace of public opinion (not unlike what our first-century brothers and sisters experienced).

Nothing New Under the Sun

As Christ-followers, we believe God has made Himself known through creation, our conscience, and special revelation in Scripture. And He has never stuttered when He has spoken, making His character crystal clear so that we wouldn't mistake Him for any other so-called gods. And two thousand years since Christianity's inception, in the midst of our culture's buffet-style theology, the church still maintains that God's identity isn't optional (or even open to a facelift).

God isn't too hip on sharing His glory.

However, pluralism is also nothing new. Way back in the Old Testament, a diverse range of religious beliefs coexisted alongside ancient, monotheistic Judaism. Baal worship and various forms of Canaanite deities crop up repeatedly throughout the Jewish record. And it was in this worldview context that God spoke, clearly setting Himself apart from other deities and distinguishing Israel from other nations. A simple read of the Old Testament and one can quickly see that God isn't too hip on sharing His glory.

> "I am the LORD; that is my name;
>   my glory I give to no other,
>   nor my praise to carved idols."
> (Isaiah 42:8)

> "My glory I will not give to another."
> (Isaiah 48:11b)

That sounds a bit narrow-minded and exclusive…maybe even egotistical or self-centered. Apparently God thinks He deserves all of humankind's adoration and praise.

All of it. How dare He?

And though Scripture claims the Lord does all things well, sharing His glory apparently isn't one of them. He is decidedly intolerant on that issue.

Interestingly, when the ancient Assyrians and Babylonians took Israel into captivity, it was largely due to the Jewish nation's worship of multiple gods, abandoning their allegiance to the one true God. Over time, it had become very fashionable to mix the worship of Yahweh with Ashtoreth and Molech, the cultural gods of Baal.

But God's intolerance of rivals isn't because He's insecure or jealous, like some middle-school girl. God's jealousy for His glory goes much deeper than mere human emotion or understanding. This guarding of His glory and an unwillingness to share the spotlight of praise is rooted in the essence of God Himself. The very nature—even the idea—of God demands that He has no peers. No equals. If the Bible is true, then Yahweh stands alone as God. Period. One Deity, existing in three Persons—Father, Son, and Holy Spirit.

> The very nature of God demands that He has no peers.

This logically means there is no such thing as Allah. No Molech. No Baal. No Krishna. These deities are, in reality, conjured up from man's religious imagination, or perhaps even manifestations of demonic entities, fallen angels masquerading as gods. And why would they do this? Could it be they want the glory too?[5]

Another reason for God's jealousy is His love for us. As God, He understands that we were made for Him alone and that our souls are never fulfilled until they are worshipping Him.

So do the logic. Either Yahweh is God or He isn't. And if He isn't, then every other religion or belief system on planet Earth is up for grabs. Like your choice of music, food, clothing, or lifestyle, it's whatever works best for you. Personal preference and experience then become the path to Paradise, not some irrefutable absolute truth about an invisible Supreme Being.

Unfortunately, this preference for pluralism didn't work out so well for the Jewish nation, resulting in painful and prolonged consequences—displacement, subjugation, and slavery. And in time, they realized God was not the syncretistic, eclectic Deity who is one of many faith options.

So let's fast-forward to today. What are people really saying when they affirm, "It doesn't really matter what you believe as long as you are sincere and treat others fairly." Does this make sense? Is it even rational?

With myriad belief systems available today, it can be both confusing and difficult as Christians paddle their way upstream against the flow. Though some postmodern theologians suggest that time and history has changed God's character and what ancient Scripture says is true of Him, the author of Hebrews (who claimed the Word of God was living)[6] maintained, "Jesus Christ is the same yesterday and today and forever."[7] And the prophet Malachi wrote, "For I the LORD do not change."[8] Since God exists outside of time, centuries of history and the advance of civilizations cannot alter His character…or cause Him to warm up to the idea of pluralism.

> According to Scripture, there is still room for only One on heaven's throne.

According to Scripture, there is still room for only One on heaven's throne.

Okay, okay, you may be thinking, *I already believe that. But does today's pluralism still personally affect me as a believer? Is it really that big of a deal? I mean, come on. Isn't it about time the church took a chill pill and relaxed?*

The Incredible Shrinking Planet

Everybody knows our world is getting smaller. Within just one generation, massive change has occurred with communication, community, and commerce. Virtually every person now possesses global access to almost anything. Someone shares a thought through a tweet, and in a few seconds people all over the world know about it. When Osama bin Laden was killed, it took just minutes before phones all over planet Earth lit up with texts, banners, emails, bulletins, and push notifications. Through the Internet, the world is literally at our fingertips. In our information-rich and technology-driven age, we are now more aware of the vastness of the universe and the world around us than any previous generation in history. You and I are a big part of that process and phenomenon.

In the religious community, a move toward a blending of religions has begun.

Additionally, reason, philosophy, and science have risen as new gods to be revered and respected while faith is considered Victorian or antiquated. Obsolete. Out of date. A relic of a time long since passed, before humanity matured. In the religious community, a move toward a blending of religions has begun. But it's not the concerted conspiracy of a particular person or religious organization. Rather, it's something much more subtle and sinister. It's almost as if it's in the air we breathe.[9]

Consequently, faith in unchanging absolute truth has been moved into the adjoining room like an unwanted old uncle at Thanksgiving dinner. And many Christians have unfortunately become products of their age, just as Paul warned against.[10] The result is that, while most Christians may flatly reject pluralism, they may still not be able to effectively defend the faith against a strong logical, philosophical, or scientific argument.

And the world continues to shrink and become one.

We find ourselves interacting with people of all sorts of faiths, philosophies, persuasions, and lifestyle choices.

The good news is that this positions us to deliver the Gospel to all nations and in large numbers. However, it's easy to post anonymous rants about our faith online, as the walls of the World Wide Web insulate us to a degree. But try it in the classroom, workplace, or in our community, and we find ourselves suddenly interacting with people of all sorts of beliefs, faiths, philosophies, backgrounds, persuasions, and lifestyle choices. They are no longer across the world. They now live across the street. They sit across the aisle at school. They work in the cubicle next to ours. These people are not our enemies. They're our neighbors and friends, those we love and care about.

Sadly, instead of demonstrating our concern for them through talking about Jesus, we often misapply the Christian values of compassion and tolerance by accepting their beliefs as "okay for them." I mean, doesn't it sound a bit arrogant to tell someone that their entire belief system (upon which they may have built their whole life) is nothing more than a big fat lie and deception? Who wants that kind of unpopularity, especially with people we like!

And yet, in our Gospel silence (perhaps due to fear or ignorance), we may unknowingly contribute toward creating a world of "customizable" beliefs. We help define truth as "whatever is true for you."

It's not the Truth that's uniting us but the belief that there is no ultimate truth.

But what would it be like if this casual approach was widely accepted in other parts of society? What if pharmacists and surgeons (or the person who writes your paycheck) operated with this relativistic approach, doing whatever "seemed right for them at the moment"? Fortunately, a commitment to unwavering accuracy still remains the standard in these fields.

And yet, when it comes to matters of faith and religion, there is no universally accepted standard or measure. It's not the Truth that's uniting us. Instead, what's bringing us together is the belief that there is no ultimate truth.

Even many ministers argue for packaging a newer, tastier Gospel that digests easier than the exclusive claims and narrow requirements of the past. As a result, our world is rapidly becoming one, with apocalyptic implications. As a planet, we have become "Post-Jesus."

Reading the Warning Signs

Okay, so just why are these issues so important? Think of it this way: Sharing your belief about who has the best college football team only makes you a loyal fan. You can argue the merits of your favorite team with others, but in the end it's just a game without any global significance or life-changing implications. But belief in who the God of the Universe is...well, not so trivial. If there is such a thing as absolute truth, then it really does matter what we believe.

To avoid being naïve Christians, we must understand how today's multifaith approach changes the way we think about the important stuff. And what exactly are the theological and practical implications of pluralism? Pluralism informs and influences a person's beliefs concerning:

The Nature of God

Like a sidewalk artist's caricatures, pluralism's portrait of God is a distorted one, with certain features highlighted (love, acceptance, compassion) while others are muted, downplayed, or completely ignored (justice, holiness, or even wrath). With a pluralistic perspective, God is not portrayed as constant but as constantly evolving, becoming better over time—reflecting culture's beliefs and us more accurately. In religion, He's a glorified Sugar Daddy, dispensing free passes to heaven like a travelling circus promoter.

The State of Humankind

Though belief is important, pluralism promotes a person's thoughts and beliefs to sovereign status. It elevates man's ideas, making them binding and authoritative. But what we think actually matters very little for determining truth. Belief cannot create truth. It can only validate it. Believing $2 + 2 = 4$ is valid only if $2 + 2$ actually equals 4. Believing that man is inherently sinful and in need of salvation is not a widely held belief. But what is this belief based on?

In the final analysis, what matters most is what God thinks and says about Himself and us. Our low view of God and disproportionately high view of man is inverted. Our thinking must reverse if we are to genuinely understand the world's need for Jesus.

The Mission of Christians

As subtle forms of pluralism creep into the Christian faith, we become missionally impotent. For why would you take the effort to share Jesus with someone if your beliefs aren't any more true or valid than theirs? Many Christians today suffer from "missional paralysis." But being bold about Christ and His claims requires a confident, courageous faith and the ability to endure what people might think about you. A tough assignment, but one worth the risk. At least the early church thought so.

Universalism

With the publication of Rob Bell's *Love Wins*, Universalism burst into the Christian conversation, uniting and dividing people from all belief spectrums. Universalism is the idea that (somehow) everyone eventually goes to heaven regardless of the object of their belief. While some closet Universalists may not be vocal about believing this for fear of being labeled heretics, secretly they still hope for that heavenly loophole where everyone makes it. We live in a time where armchair theologians (preachers, authors, bloggers) have emerged, unfurling a banner that effectively reads, "There is no hell. Everyone will eventually be saved. We are all one…at last." This is the logical result of religious pluralistic thinking.

Our Doubts

Religious pluralism in culture has also created many secret doubters in the church. For this reason, we're forced to reexamine some foundational questions about our faith, such as: "Do people of all religions really need Jesus in order to get into heaven? Do they require Christ in order to be declared righteous in God's sight?"

What chance do we have of dodging doubt in a world filled with thousands of conflicting beliefs?

If Jesus' own cousin, John the Baptist, a man who spent his entire life preparing for Christ and promoting Him, could experience major doubts on his deathbed about whether Jesus was the true Messiah, what chance do we have of dodging doubt in a world filled with thousands of conflicting beliefs?

Having doubts or questioning isn't a bad thing. It's what you do with those doubts that makes the difference. We shouldn't ignore the hard questions. Instead, we have to seek answers and think about why we believe what we believe.

Doubt isn't foreign to Scripture and its strugglers (Abraham, Thomas, Peter, and many more doubted). The real question is, "When God's words and ways seem confusing or troubling to my thinking, emotions, and nature, can He still be trusted?"

Do you suppose Abraham experienced some inner turmoil at the thought of Sodom and Gomorrah being destroyed? And yet, even in his confusion, he posed the question, "Shall not the Judge of all the earth do what is just?"[11] The psalmist declared, "[God] will judge the peoples with equity."[12] And a few verses later writes, "He will judge the world in righteousness, and the peoples in his faithfulness."[13]

So ask the hard questions, but keep moving forward. Confidence comes to those who diligently seek God while submitting to His character and justice. Only then can we honestly face and overcome our doubts.

> Confidence comes to those who diligently seek God while submitting to His character and justice.

Tolerance as the New Truth

As the pool of beliefs deepens and widens in our culture, the more narrow- and closed-minded the cultural perception of Christians. And it's not going to get better. Today, tolerance is the newest god in the marketplace, easily obtained through trading in our conviction about biblical truth.

Tolerance can be good and bad. It can be good when it means that we are patient with one another, when we bear with one anothers' weaknesses, when we lovingly care for one another in spite of our differences, and when we seek to understand one another. This kind of tolerance is a Christian virtue every believer should strive for.

Tolerance is bad when a Christian succumbs to the lie that he is a bigot if he defends his beliefs and values in the public square. Even those who claim there are no absolute values will still vehemently defend the (absolute) value of tolerance. Christians unwilling to bow to this god are routinely labeled as mean-spirited "fanatics" and "haters" (and some are). But all this is merely evidence of a rising tide of subtle persecution that will one day swell to tsunami proportions.

How ironic that "open-minded" atheists often promote intolerance and even hostility toward those who claim God exists. Relativists contradict themselves by saying it doesn't matter what you believe, but then condemn the belief in the absolute truth of God. They quickly turn on you, because the only absolute truth for them is the truth that there is no absolute truth. To disagree with them is to encounter intolerance and hatred.

> God is either the God depicted in the Bible or He isn't.

Obviously, not all beliefs can be true. Not all roads lead to God, because many of these belief systems flatly contradict one another. While it's possible for two belief systems to both be wrong, they can't both be right. God cannot at the same time both exist (theism) and not exist (atheism). Atheism and Christianity cannot both be right. It's impossible. A logical contradiction. God either is or He isn't. He is either the God depicted in the Bible or He isn't. Pluralism is therefore a classic contradiction. It doesn't work—logically, philosophically, or theologically.

Something has to be true. If we say nothing is true then we are living in an illusion and the illusion becomes our invalid reality. As Christians, we claim Jesus is that truth. We believe the world is genuinely in trouble and that people really do need a Savior. We believe Christ came to us and died for the sins we could never atone for. We believe He bridged the gap between man and God through His death and resurrection.

But because we're fallen humans, we're naturally turned off by some of God's words, especially those that make us uncomfortable. Jesus' exclusive claims fall into that category. It's not natural for us to accept Him or His words. His truth doesn't sit well with our theological tastebuds. Some of God's truth is palatable and comforting, but at other times it's distasteful and hard to digest. This becomes both a challenge and an opportunity to exercise faith and humility in our relationship with Him. I suspect this falls into the "I'm God and you're not" category.

Did Jesus Believe in Jesus?

Popular thinking would reinvent Jesus as a soft-spoken hipster-poet promoting world peace and coexistence among the world's religions. And while it's true that Christianity united Jew and Gentile, rich and poor under a common belief and family, Jesus' own words and actions often divided people more than uniting them. In our day, where absolute (or propositional) truth is viewed as repressive, narrow-minded, and mean-spirited, Jesus' claims stand out more than ever. Perhaps nowhere is this more evident than in His most often-quoted declaration. With two short sentences, the Sage from Nazareth drew a timeless, definitive line in the sand. Speaking to His soon-to-become-famous doubting disciple, Jesus replied to Thomas concerning the path to heaven,

> "I am the way, and the truth, and the life. No one comes
> to the Father except through Me."[14]

Statements such as this cause adherents of pluralism to scatter in fear like cockroaches in a newly lit room.

As with His other statements, Jesus knew exactly what He was saying. His words were confident and designed to communicate exclusivity. He knew who He was, where He had come from, and where He was going. He was fully convinced of His identity and

Jesus knew who He was, where He had come from, and where He was going.

mission and that access to heaven was His alone to grant. This bold claim is brazen and arrogant...if it's not true. And He risked offending not only those who heard Him speak it, but all of humanity.

But Jesus would have been a complete fool to get Himself crucified if there was any other way to heaven. What kind of person hangs bleeding on a cross in unimaginable agony for a lark or a lie? One must concede, even if they don't believe in Jesus, that Jesus believed in Jesus. He believed He was the only way. In fact, the night before He was arrested, tortured, and crucified, He prayed, begging the Father for another way.[15] His humanity cried out for God's infinite mind to think up some other divine strategy to redeem this rebel human race. In the garden He seemingly asked, "Is there another way?"

But heaven gave no answer.

If God could have devised another path to salvation, don't you think He would have chosen it?

Shortly afterward, strengthened by an angel,[16] He would rise from prayer and begin His painful journey to the cross. And why? Because He believed fully there was no other way. You could claim Jesus was deluded or insane, but that wouldn't match the nature of His words, actions, character, and the testimony of those who knew Him best. It also fails to account for the untold millions of lives He's changed. If God, in His infinite wisdom, could have devised another path to salvation, don't you think He would have chosen it? But the Father gave no other option. A multitude of religious efforts or human options falls short. Even the Old Testament Law was inadequate to solve our sin problem. Only Jesus could pay the penalty for our sin by drinking the cup of God's wrath.

Only Jesus did it.

Perhaps you've secretly wondered, *But what about now? Now that God has had more time to think about it, now that there are good people in all religions and lifestyle choices, is there still no other way?*

What if someone sincerely believes in You with all their heart, but just happens to call You by another religion's name?
Wouldn't You accept them then?

But belief itself never causes anything to be true or untrue, valid or bogus. Beliefs become legit when they reflect truth. You can believe with all your heart that the chair you're sitting in can take you to New York, but your belief doesn't make it true. You can believe in aliens or the Easter Bunny, but your belief doesn't make them any more real. What we believe is irrelevant unless it's grounded in fact. It's the object of a person's belief that's important. Place your faith in the right object and suddenly your belief has purpose, meaning, power, and validity.

> What we believe is irrelevant unless it's grounded in fact.

Similarly, when it comes to heaven, a person's belief is only credible if it is placed in a credible object. Jesus Christ claimed to be that credible object. He claimed to be "the way and the truth." And either He is or He isn't. It's that simple.

From Clarity to Confidence

So where does that leave us? As we've said, at its core, Christianity is defined by the belief that Jesus is both the Christ and the Lord. God in human flesh. He alone, through His undeniable death and resurrection, connects humankind to God. People don't get martyred for pluralism. Jesus' disciples spilled their blood because they believed the world really needed *only* Him.

Do we believe as they did?

In the end, pluralism is a false belief, a subtle lie pressuring Christians to weaken their defense of the faith. As a result, the Gospel is diluted because of fear and an attempt to keep peace with our culture. Even in our churches, we must always guard against becoming a social club or being caught up in programs and events, and then hyping those events with creativity in an attempt to win the world to Christ.

We can try so hard to relate to the world that we become virtually indistinguishable from it. We can't simply imitate culture and by this effort expect to reach it. We won't change people's hearts because of our innovation, creativity, or technology, or because of our political influence. We also won't reach the world by shunning all things secular and isolating ourselves from culture. Jesus wouldn't want that.[17]

So, in an increasingly pluralistic age that desperately needs help, hope, and Jesus, what are we to do? How are we to live? If following Christ is really worth it, then how can we clearly and convincingly demonstrate this reality? And will anyone even notice?

If lobbing Gospel grenades at a pagan culture won't do it...

If retreating into the safety of the church walls won't do it...

If absorbing culture with its values won't do it...

If slick, amazing presentations and church services won't do it...then what will?

Let's find out.

GOSPEL APPEALS

- *Before you worry about standing out for Jesus, first learn to sit before Him.*
- *Watch how you live, because others are.*
- *Jesus was willing to die for you. Are you willing to live for Him?*

Questions for Further Thought and Discussion

1. Are you a Fifth-Gospel Christian? That's a big question. Why is it so important to be able to answer this question in the affirmative?

2. Considering that most people will never read the first four Gospels, what needs to change in your life for you to be a Fifth-Gospel Christian?

3. How can pluralism weaken one's obedience to the command to share Christ?

4. Why is this "Jesus is the only way" language so hard to digest in today's culture?

5. Bobby said, "People don't get martyred for pluralism." Do you agree with this statement? Why or why not?

6. If Jesus wasn't the only way to heaven, why would He have been a fool to die for our sins?

Chapter 2

IMAGE IS EVERYTHING

*"I like your Christ. I do not like your Christians.
Your Christians are so unlike your Christ."*

MOHANDAS GANDHI

When Jesus exited our planet around 30 AD, He left His disciples in charge to mind the store. It was their mission, as it is ours, to accurately reflect our Lord to the world. We've already seen that people generally have a skewed mental portrait of God. And, for better or worse, that perception is largely formed by their interaction with Christians. Their opinions sometimes do overlap with the truth. But true or not, people's personal views about Jesus and His followers really matter, and here's why: *They matter because they tell us how clearly we are representing God and communicating His message.*

Any good speaker or writer will tell you it's their job as a communicator to convey their ideas clearly. If the audience fails to get it, then (humanly speaking) the communicator is responsible. And God has called us to responsibly model Jesus to our world.

Mirror, Mirror...?

But let's call a brief time-out here and admit that "being Jesus" to the world can be an intimidating task for which we feel woefully inadequate.

Agreed?

God understands this too. And that's why He's so fiercely committed to your sanctification (probably not a word you've used in conversation this past week, but it's nevertheless an intensely important biblical term).[1] Practically defined, sanctification is God's ongoing work of transforming you into Christlikeness from the inside out. It's God making His image clearly reflect through you over time. *Sanctification* originally meant "to be set apart," and came to signify being set apart in character and lifestyle. It means our lives have the unique signature of God on them, that we are different. Not different as in weird, but different as in revealing Christ and His love.

Though we were originally created in God's image,[2] God's reflection in us was marred in the Garden of Eden when Adam and Eve sinned. And though His image wasn't completely erased, it was defaced and tarnished. When you trusted in Christ, the Holy Spirit began the beautiful work of "image restoration" in you, masterfully remaking you to more accurately reflect God's virtue. He began sculpting, forming, and transforming your character to better display Christ to the world. You become His image-bearer, and His ongoing work in your life distinguishes you from the world. This is a lifelong process, by the way, and one God is committed to completing.[3]

Some people resist Christ because...well, they know some Christians.

Previously scarred by sin, you and I now have the opportunity to represent our Creator to His creation. So it makes sense that when nonbelievers see us as lifeless, unchanged, empty, or abrasive, they not only wonder why our lives look just like theirs, but they may also conclude our God doesn't even exist. At all. Plainly stated, some people resist Christ because…well, they know some Christians.

Insert sad face here.

None of us will ever perfectly represent God's character. As long as we're on this earth, we'll have imperfections. And it's these imperfections that some unbelievers are quick (and happy) to point out and expose. But there is value in listening to what others say, of taking an honest look in the mirror, of stepping into an unbeliever's shoes to see what they perceive about Jesus and His bride. Think of it as a spiritual awareness-building exercise.

My intention isn't to join the angry mob and engage in the popular sport of Christian bashing. There's plenty of that out there. Nor do I offer some sort of an apology in hopes of persuading the world to finally like us. Rather, my intention is to honestly and responsibly reclaim God's reputation in this world.

The Good

While the church has dropped the ball, we must not forget what an example the church has been to many in our world, especially through its acts of service. Think about the good done in the name of Christianity: The first orphanages were run by churches. The church and Christians founded many of the great American universities, including Harvard, Princeton, and Yale. The church was pivotal in leading society to abolish slavery with leaders like William Wilberforce. George Williams created the YMCA in order to protect youth from the hazardous conditions on the streets. William Booth founded the Salvation Army to care for the poor and disadvantaged. Millard and Linda Fuller started Habitat for Humanity to provide housing internationally for the poor. Even today, many churches are passionate in their attempt to help the homeless, protect women from abortion, and to end the spread of HIV/AIDS.

Becoming a true reflection of Christ to the world begins with a healthy dose of humility and introspection.

This list is a mere sampling of how the church has shined through the ages. However, as commendable as these acts of service are, if our character isn't intact for Christ, we will look like any other philanthropy. There's still a lot of work in our world to be done, and it starts with you and me.

The Bad and the Ugly

Many years ago a newspaper posed the question, "What's wrong with the world?" Wordsmith G.K. Chesterton immediately fired back a letter to the paper with this response:

> Dear Sirs:
>
> I am.
>
> Sincerely yours,
> G.K. Chesterton

Becoming a true reflection of Christ to the world begins with a healthy dose of humility and introspection. It starts by taking a look within and realizing our continued, desperate need for Christ. It includes admitting we all need a little image work, and in some cases, perhaps a lot.

How the World Perceives Us

So what do they really think of us out there, beyond the church walls? Where have we missed the mark in showing the world who God really is? What do they believe about us? See if any of the following perspectives from non-Christians ring true.

Brian—"Christians are so divisive. Why can't you guys get along?"

Recently, while in the waiting area at Tire Kingdom, I began a conversation with a man. As we talked, he revealed to me that (according to his faith) he was god (face-palm…and I had no idea I was sitting beside god all this time!). I've had some bizarre conversations with people while sharing my faith, but I'd never physically met god before. I was surprised how much Scripture he actually knew—out of context of course.

When I attempted to talk with him about Christ, he became very resistant, saying, "There are over 30,000 Christian denominations, so how can you possibly claim to have the truth?" I counterargued his claim, but he persisted. "Look it up if you like." So I did, and to my surprise he underestimated! One website contends there are 43,257 denominations, and the number is rising.[4]

One website contends there are 43,257 denominations, and the number is rising.

This was hard to swallow and even harder to digest. Granted, some of these denominations may not fit within orthodox Christianity, but they all would claim their original roots in Christianity. This guy was essentially saying, "How can I believe you when there's so much division in your church? Why do you people disagree so much?"

Excellent question. Granted, some of these divisions are due to methodology rather than theology (e.g., traditional versus contemporary services, suit and dresses versus jeans and Converse, liturgical versus nonliturgical, light shows and dried ice versus stained glass). But to many, this amounts to a mixed message. Add to this stories of churches splitting because the piano player had an affair with the worship guy with a fohawk or churches engaging in heated arguments over whether to build a new building.

More often, though, these differences find their roots in nonessential theological issues, such as the timing of Jesus' return to earth or the mode of baptism. Most divisions are petty and personal, while others do deal with more weighty matters. And to a watching world, that can create tension...and confusion.

We must work to find common ground, rallying around the things in our faith that really matter.

Paul urged believers to "maintain the unity of the Spirit in the bond of peace."[5] To his Philippian friends, he passionately pleaded, "complete my joy by being of the same mind, having the same love, being in full accord and of one mind."[6] He commanded the Colossians to "put on love, which binds everything together in perfect harmony."[7] Diversity in some areas is to be embraced and celebrated, as there will always be differences between us. That's okay. But we must work to find common ground, rallying around the things in our faith that really matter.[8] This kind of unity enhances God's reputation outside the church.

Of course no one can change God's character. As John Wooden, the legendary UCLA basketball coach once said, "Your character is what you really are, while your reputation is merely what others think you are." It's a sizable burden to realize the church holds some responsibility for God's reputation in the world and what others say about Him.

Sarah—"Christians are such buzz kills. You're no fun!"

Some perceive Jesus' followers as killjoys. We're boring, uncool, and against everything fun and pleasurable. Some of this, of course, depends on your definition of "fun and pleasurable." But are we really guilty as charged? Maybe a better question would be, are we showing non-Christians the real Christ?

God the Father says of Jesus,

> "You have loved righteousness and hated wickedness;
> therefore God, your God, has anointed you
>   with the oil of gladness beyond your companions."[9]

No one understood joy and gladness more than Jesus Christ. And why? According to this verse, it was because He "loved righteousness and hated wickedness." Jesus was sinless and, as a result, guiltless. Any mental-health professional will tell you that guilt robs people of their joy.

Jesus was joy personified, and He births that same joy in those who follow Him.

Guilt makes us miserable and paralyzes us spiritually. But Jesus was guilt-free and joy-full. Contrary to what many believe, walking in grace-centered righteousness is what produces real, lasting joy. And Jesus Christ perfectly modeled that full life of abundance. He celebrated and enjoyed life.[10] And He knew unimaginable joy awaited Him in heaven.[11]

So Jesus was far from being a killjoy. He was joy personified, and He births that same joy in those who follow Him. When we understand what it means to have been "declared righteous," we can expect to find a similar overflow of joy. Admittedly, there are pleasures and fun apart from God, but at best they are temporary and ultimately unfulfilling.[12]

Being a Christian doesn't exempt us from difficult life experiences and hard times, but even in the midst of them we can still experience joy. That's why James could confidently write, "Count it all joy, my brothers, when you meet trials of various kinds."[13] And it's this very joy that can be so attractive to others. Joy is like a magnet and hard to ignore. There's no room or reason for overly serious, soured followers of Jesus who throw hissy fits when Christians play Uno. For these people, it's as if every day is Judgment Day. They look depressed, angry, and empty. Who wants that? I don't!

Claire—"Christians are separatists. They live in their own little Christian bubbles."

During the fifth century, there was this dude named Simeon Stylites. Nice name, huh? Simeon was a pole sitter (you probably don't know many pole sitters, do you?). This Simeon lived a strict life of asceticism in Syria, literally sitting atop a stone pillar some fifty feet high. And he did this for thirty-nine years without coming down. Not even a bungee jump. Thirty-nine years! And there he sat in his unbathed condition atop that pillar, "separated" from the world for nearly four decades.

Not surprisingly, his accomplishment stands strong in the *Guinness Book of World Records*. (So that's what you want to be remembered for, Simeon? I bet your parents were proud.) And yet some have called Simeon a saint. Honestly, I think the guy was pretty stupid. I mean, why would anyone do that? Simeon attempted to show everyone how separated he was from the world. That he was closer to heaven, away from those down on the earth. Following his death in 459 AD, other Christian ascetics followed his example, also becoming pole sitters.

Many Christians feel more saintly by obeying a long list of don'ts while failing to do what God called them to do.

Lemmings.

Of course, church history is no stranger to separatism. From pillar hermits to monastic monks to modern-day separatists who avoid contact with unbelievers, Pharisaism is alive and well. You probably won't spend your life sitting on a pole, but like Simeon, many Christians today feel more saintly by obeying a long list of don'ts while failing to do what God called them to do—to go "and make disciples of all nations."[14]

Like the fear-mongering religious elite of Jesus' day, these people believe contact with culture somehow contaminates you. But again, on His final night here, Jesus prayed for us to be insulated not isolated.[15] And there is a difference.

The church Christ birthed was commissioned to infiltrate and influence culture, not separate from it. But because of modern-day Pharisees posing as believers, many choose to reject Christ.

Darin—"Christians are so hateful. Why are you people so mean?"

Making judgments is an unavoidable part of daily life. The light turns yellow and we judge whether to stop or go. We watch a film and we judge whether we like the characters, the plot, the storyline, the cinematography. We watch a singer on *The Voice* and judge whether their performance appeals to us. We see a man sporting eyeliner and think, *Hmm.*

People are okay with that kind of judgment. But they draw the line with moral judgments. If a Christian takes a stand on a moral issue, they are labeled "hateful and judgmental." To be fair, there actually are mean-spirited Christians, but unfortunately this criticism extends to any believer who dares to disagree with accepted (im)morality.

But here's the big difference between making judgments and being judgmental. Judgmentalism communicates pride and condescension, with the world often feeling the impact of our hurled stones instead of our love.

> There's a big difference between making judgments and being judgmental.

From God's perspective, there is both an unwise and a wise approach to judgment. For example, in His Sermon on the Mount, Jesus warned against condemning others for the things we also do.[16] That's straight up hypocrisy. Judgment becomes a problem when we self-righteously condemn people while simultaneously doing the very things we're judging them for. Jesus says, "Don't do that." This turns us into blind judges. We can't correct in others what we've failed to correct in ourselves. For the authentic Christian, there is no such thing as a superiority complex. Hateful or hypocritical condemnation always saddens God's heart.

But Jesus also never intended His followers to be moral wimps. We can still say with confidence that murder, rape, and robbery are morally wrong. But isn't that judging? Sure it is, but this kind of judgment involves a moral discernment based on God's objective standards. And we, like God, can make those judgments while still feeling compassion and love for others. This kind of judgment avoids hateful words, emotions, or feelings of superiority. Simply agreeing with God and His standards while disagreeing with someone else does not equal hatred. It's very possible to disagree without being disagreeable. Jesus didn't teach us not to judge; He taught us *how* to judge, biblically.

Jerrod—"Christians are fake, plastic people in a pretend world."

Although there is such a thing as a fake Christian, a Christian fake is an oxymoron. In fact, no person should be more real and authentic than a follower of Jesus. Because the gift of salvation has secured our standing with God, Christians have been endowed with the very best sense of self. Growing believers are more aware every day of how desperate they are for Christ. Because of our sensitivity to God's holiness and our own sin, we believers can be most

Knowing Christ is the key to authenticity.

in touch with what is real. The Gospel brings us face to face with ourselves and real life like nothing else. It births and breathes authenticity...naturally.

Knowing Christ is the key to this authenticity. Though we may often devolve into plastic versions of ourselves, God wants to introduce us instead to our true identity. Christianity begins with a confession of what is real—our sin and Jesus as Savior. But if we ignore our post-salvation spiritual struggle and growth, we end up hiding behind an illusion of false religiosity. And people detect this and conclude, "I can't relate to that."

But imagine if nonbelievers saw the church as broken people still needing God's everyday help? What if, instead of trying to appear better, we were simply grateful for being better off in Christ?

What if others began to see us as fellow strugglers who are real and transparent about our lives and families? This kind of authenticity means admitting we're still in process, and that without Jesus, there is nothing good about us.[17] That's a refreshing alternative to being fake and artificial, isn't it?

Ashley—"Christians are hypocrites. They're two-faced."

This is true...partially. There are some pretenders out there, and they are pretty easy to spot. Some of these folks are actual Christians and some aren't. Some are living in willful disobedience to God, while others are infant believers who haven't yet learned to walk. But the fact remains—some Christians talk one way and act another. They pretend to be something they're not. They're not the real deal. They're actors.

It's both comforting and convicting to note that Jesus hated hypocrisy, reserving His most scathing rebukes for religious people who weren't genuinely spiritual on the inside.

But hypocrites are everywhere—at school, college, church, work, the hospital, a football game, the grocery store, in politics, and in your neighborhood. It's naïve to think other religions and belief systems don't also have their share of hypocrites—those whose public persona is devout while they are anything but in private.

So Christianity is not exclusively guilty of hypocrisy. Humanity is. Another way of putting it is hypocrisy isn't a Christian problem; it's a human problem. Wherever you find people, you will encounter hypocrisy in varying degrees. All humans are depraved and sinful, with natures as deceitful as evil itself.[18] Even those who condemn Christian hypocrisy do not perfectly live up to their own philosophy, moral code, or religious standards.

> Hypocrisy isn't a Christian problem; it's a human problem.

So how would you respond to a friend who accused Christians of being hypocrites? Here's some seasoned, practical advice. First, acknowledge that hypocrisy exists. Second, understand that just because a person acts hypocritically from time to time, it doesn't mean they are full-time hypocrites. Good, sincere people fail. A lot. Including Christians. And yes, including me. Third, agree that hypocrisy is offensive and wrong, and since Jesus condemned it, those who are repulsed by it have this in common with Him. Fourth, if someone is counterfeiting spiritual integrity and true godliness, it only proves there is a corresponding reality. While hypocrites are bad PR for God and Christianity, this only demonstrates the authenticity of the Christian faith. A counterfeit twenty-dollar bill isn't bogus unless there is also a corresponding legal-tender twenty-dollar bill. Fifth, tell your friend you're sorry that Christians have hurt or disappointed him. But challenge him not to judge the whole based only on a few. One scene doesn't have to ruin the whole movie. And lastly, encourage your skeptical or jaded friends to join you and other imperfect people in pursuit of the truth.

Matt—"Christians don't care about me. They only want me to become a Christian."

When I became a believer, I unintentionally turned my family off to God. I was so in their face about their need to repent and turn to Jesus that, for a season, I actually turned them away from Jesus. Then one night my brother Tim and I were sitting in a hot tub at a friend's condominium. Another person joined us, and I began talking to him about Christ. By the time we were finished, he was ready to place his faith in Jesus Christ. Right there in the hot tub this guy trusted Christ, my brother observing the whole episode. When we left later that evening, Tim said, "Bobby, when you prayed to lead that guy to Christ, I want you to know that I trusted Christ as well."

I couldn't believe it. What had happened? Tim had previously been resistant to the Gospel. He then admitted, "For the first time I was actually able to get the Gospel because I didn't feel like you were just preaching at me."

My brother went on to experience a major life change. Today, he's an active part of our church, a lover of Jesus. He just needed his brother to care about him as a person, not just his salvation.

Jesus calls His followers to risk and adventure, to engage those who are not like us.

It's important to remind ourselves that God rarely operates on our timetable. As we've heard it said many times before, "People don't care how much we know until they know how much we care." Trite as that statement may sound, it's true. And we are successful when we simply share Christ and leave the results to God.

Reflecting God's image often means reaching out to people who aren't like us. If you want to reach those who already agree with you on moral and political issues, then your reach will be very limited. But Jesus calls His followers to risk and adventure, to engage those who are not like us. Changing someone's view on a moral issue (such as homosexuality, abortion, drugs) does absolutely nothing to get him or her closer to heaven. A homosexual or drug addict may stop their immoral activity but still not become righteous in God's sight. Salvation isn't a matter of moral behavior, otherwise any "good" person could strive for it.

This is not to say that important issues shouldn't be discussed or debated, but rather that they aren't critical for salvation. The most important topic of salvation is Jesus—who He is and what He has done for us.

Agreed, there is often some pre-witnessing work to be done, removing potential obstacles that keep others from listening to Christ's message. For example, you can have some healthy discussions if someone says,

- "I'm an atheist, so I don't believe in your God. In fact, I think He is like a childhood imaginary friend you made up to keep you company and give you comfort."

- "I believe in evolution."

- "I don't trust the reliability of the Bible. I think they just made up all that stuff about Jesus after He died."

- "Christians are against women's rights. I can't tolerate a religion that is full of sexism and bigotry."

- "Christians hate gays. I believe God accepts everyone."

Showing the World Who Jesus Really Is

So how are you supposed to show Jesus to people like this, since their opinions are strong and are held by the majority of contemporary society?

Train Ourselves to Think Biblically

First, we have to train ourselves to think biblically not emotionally. According to Scripture, all people are "dead in sin," incapable of coming to Christ apart from God's work in them.[19]

Even if someone agrees with you regarding creation, abortion, or homosexuality, that doesn't mean they are more spiritually alive than an atheist, murderer, or Satan worshipper. Salvation is an act of God, not a slow climb to heaven through our intellectual, moral, philosophical, or spiritual efforts. If someone agrees with you politically, it may mean that's a battle you won't have to fight (though political issues carry no saving weight with God). But it doesn't mean they are any more likely to trust in Christ and follow Him. So first know what Scripture says and let it inform and guide your thinking.

Understand What the World Believes

Second, at times it may be wise to postpone sharing Jesus if you can have a rational, civil discussion about an issue that is keeping someone from listening about Christ. But for that to happen, you need to know your stuff. While most people can't rationally and logically defend their beliefs (no matter what they may be), occasionally you will encounter an atheist or skeptic who presents strong arguments in support of their views. The issues and mindset of our times requires us to be informed believers. So study up. Ask them to give you reasons why they believe the way they do. Let them present their case, if they are able. Are their views grounded in history, philosophy, and fact or mere emotions and prejudice? If you are unable to respond confidently, then get back to them when you are more prepared and equipped. And remember, there is no shame in simply saying, "I don't know."

Above all, focus on being an expert in God's truth and love.

People aren't argued into salvation, but that doesn't mean you shouldn't be informed and educated. It also doesn't mean you can't have healthy, vibrant discussions or debates. Just keep in mind that (ultimately) it's God's sovereign power, truth, and love that changes a life. Above all, focus on being an expert in His truth and love.

Allow God's Holy Spirit to do the internal arguing and convincing for you.[20]

Bottom line: We depend on the supernatural work of God, not on our persuasive abilities.

The Bible says concerning unbelievers, "The natural person does not accept the things of the Spirit of God, for they are folly to him, and he is not able to understand them because they are spiritually discerned."[21] When you combine a Christian blinded by pride with an unbeliever blinded to the truth, you have a lose-lose situation. The blind leading the blind. God wants us to submit to His Spirit[22] and to trust Him to open the eyes of the spiritually blind. But sometimes we have to show a little extra effort in displaying humility for our unbelieving friends.

Love God and People

Above all else, God desires our love for Him and others. Jesus said, "he who is forgiven little, loves little."[23] He spoke this after forgiving a sinful woman who had anointed His feet with expensive perfume. She was crushed over her sinfulness and recognized Christ's greatness. The religious crowd didn't appreciate Jesus allowing such a women to wash His feet, but He put the self-righteous leaders in their place saying, "her sins, which are many, are forgiven—for she loved much."[24]

That's a life-changing principle for us. It's only when the reality of God's forgiveness sinks into our hearts that we are free to love God and others. Only those who have truly experienced love can give love. And when the world is loved well, they won't conclude that we think we're better. And that helps us display God's image to them.

A deep romance with Jesus Christ must be our greatest passion and pursuit.

People are observing us. They want to know if what we have is real. And being real and authentic isn't achieved through rule keeping, slick presentations, or persuasive arguments, but through loving God and being loved by Him. The world has to see that we have no other higher love. It has to see that God is our life passion.

Our problem isn't ultimately about image; it's about romance. A deep romance with Jesus Christ must be our greatest passion and pursuit. If we are in love with our God, people will notice. Right now, we desperately need a generation of believers whose hearts are on fire with love for Him. This kind of love causes God to shine through us to a watching world.

In this way, we become a clear portrait of the One who loves them, God's chosen instrument to show this world what our Savior is really like.

His image. Through you. Imagine that!

GOSPEL APPEALS

- *Ultimately, we don't have an image problem—we have a romance problem.*

- *Remember, image bearing begins by building intimacy with Christ.*

- *The most satisfied people in the world are those who savor the Savior.*

- *Those who delight in God are Christianity's best branders.*

Questions for Further Thought and Discussion

1. Gandhi said, "I like your Christ. I do not like your Christians. Your Christians are so unlike your Christ." Do you think this is a common thought among nonbelievers? Why or why not?

2. Jesus prayed for our oneness so the world will know we are His disciples. This appears to be His unanswered prayer. What's it going to take for the church to model a unified front, and what will be the consequences if the church fails to figure this out?

3. How can the church show the world that it's not boring being a Christian without seeking to adopt the ways of the world?

4. Why bother having good arguments for the Christian faith if people aren't argued into being Christians?

5. Bobby said, "Ultimately, our problem isn't really about image. It's about romance. A deep romance with Jesus Christ. That must be our greatest passion and pursuit. If we are in love with our God, people will notice." What's the deal with romance? Does this really have anything to do with image reconstruction?

6. Of the different objections people have against Christianity, which one do you think is the most prevalent in our culture today? And getting real with each other, which of the objections could you be accused of?

7. Someone once said, "If you were accused of being a Christian, would there be enough evidence to prove it?" What say you?

Chapter 3

COUNTING THE COST

"When Christ calls a man, he bids him come and die."
DIETRICH BONHOEFFER

"We must do something about the cross, and one of two things only we can do—flee it or die upon it."
A.W. TOZER

In October of 2011, I flew to India to train church planters who were ministering to some unreached people groups throughout the world. Since becoming a Christian, I had read about the persecution of believers. But it wasn't until I arrived in this little Indian village that I met people who were physically beaten for the sake of the Gospel.

Trying to compare persecution in American to that in certain parts of India is like comparing a sniffle to pancreatic cancer. I showed up in this small village and learned that people walked the dusty, potholed roads for miles just to hear truth from God's Word each week. As I entered the church building, I immediately noticed the men and women were seated on a concrete floor on opposite sides of the room. There were no chairs. No air-conditioning. No baby grand piano. No coffee shop. No electric guitars. No Bose sound system and certainly no slicked-out light show to aid the musicians. Just hungry hearts for Jesus! For hours they worshipped and praised God.

Ready to Die for the Gospel

During my time in this village, I learned that fourteen local men had been beaten for sharing the Gospel. I had the privilege of meeting a few of them. One of them, a brand-new convert, was told he would have his hands and feet cut off, kerosene poured on him and his family, and then they would be set on fire. All he had to do to avoid this horrific torture was to renounce his faith in Christ.

I'd read about stuff like this and watched documentaries. I even own a copy of *Foxe's Book of Martyrs*. But now I was there. Live and in person. As I wondered how this young man could handle these awful threats, my Indian friend Benny said to me, "Bobby, he's ready to die for the Gospel."

I was overcome with deep respect and felt unworthy to teach this young man or any of these humble-hearted village people anything. Such courage moved me. What could a young white male who grew up in the affluent state of California possibly say to these people? Pausing to pray for these persecuted Christians, my eyes filled with tears and I silently wept, longing to be alone and release the tears I tried so hard to hold back.

Until that moment, I had never felt the gravity of my call to preach the Gospel the way I did that day in India. As I stood to teach those precious villagers, I said to myself, *You better be sure you believe this thing, because you're not in America anymore*. I realized my teaching may very well send these people to their death. Because they counted the cost, I was motivated to do the same.

This young convert had counted the cost and concluded that Jesus was worth it.

Back home in the States, I meet many Christians ready to live for Jesus. But how many are ready to lose their hands and feet for their Savior? This young convert had counted the cost and concluded that Jesus was worth it.

Just before being put to death under Hitler's regime on April 9, 1945, Dietrich Bonhoeffer, pastor, theologian, and author of *The Cost of Discipleship*, wrote, "When Christ calls a man, he bids him come and die."[1] Jesus put it this way, "If anyone would come after me, let him deny himself and take up his cross daily and follow me."[2] In today's language, it'd be like saying, "Take up your electric chair and follow me." Jesus was saying, "Consider the cost. Consider what it means to call yourself My disciple. Daily." He knew only legit disciples could withstand the pressure that would soon mount against those early believers. Only authentic believers would truly be able to make it as Fifth-Gospel Christians.

Failing to count the cost leads to compromise, complacency, and caving in to the enemy. Jesus calls His followers to set their priorities straight, beckoning them to stand out. But as we know, those first disciples misunderstood Him, fumbling over His words. And often their messy lives sent mixed messages. But when all was said and done, eleven of the twelve would die martyrs' deaths.

> Failing to count the cost leads to compromise, complacency, and caving in to the enemy.

The word *martyr* means "witness." As the church spread throughout the first century, Christians were beheaded, crucified, eaten by lions, torn apart, and dipped in tar to be burned at the stake as human torches.

And we complain about the church service running a few minutes late.

During a trip to Italy, I walked through the catacombs, the underground caverns outside of Rome that became the burial spots of some ten generations of Christians who spilled their blood over a three-hundred-year period. Archaeologists estimate that anywhere between 175,000 and 400,000 Christians were interred in these dark Roman tunnels. Visitors to those tombs are humbled by the Christian symbols hand-chiseled there—a fish, an anchor, a cross. Simple statements declaring the history-altering faith and witness of these early Christians. Of course, being a Fifth-Gospel Christian doesn't mean you'll necessarily die for your faith, but it does mean you must die to your life. It's only when we die to ourselves that the world can see Jesus living through us.

> Oddly enough, self-denial is the secret to self-fulfillment.

But what concerns me is that the church is seldom being challenged to count the cost. Jesus' words can be hard to digest, but they aren't without promise. Jesus also said, "For whoever would save his life will lose it, but whoever loses his life for my sake will save it."[3] Oddly enough, it turns out that self-denial is the secret to self-fulfillment. Go figure. As we follow Jesus Christ, the Gospel is formed in our lives. Our very life becomes Good News in a bad news world. It's through relinquishing our right to rule that our lives are made different. It's through surrender that we're made ready to be bearers of this Good News.

Diluted Discipleship

Bishop J.C. Ryle once said, "Nothing causes so much backsliding as enlisting disciples without letting them know what they are taking in hand." On one occasion, Jesus told a large crowd, "For which of you, desiring to build a tower, does not first sit down and *count the cost*, whether he has enough to complete it? Otherwise, when he has laid a foundation and is not able to finish, all who see it begin to mock him, saying, 'This man began to build and was not able to finish.'"[4]

And what happens to the person who fails to count the cost of following Jesus? According to Him, people "begin to mock." And isn't that how many people perceive the church today? All words and no action? A mediocre bunch of talkers? Or worse, no words and no action? Lots of church members have raised their hands, gotten their Jesus tattoo, walked an aisle, recited a sinner's prayer, and even eaten their Testamints. But have they really counted the cost? Have they seriously considered what it means to follow Jesus in our world? This love-boat Christianity isn't gonna cut it. Jesus didn't call us to a candyland Christianity, but to a count the cost Christianity.

Failing to count the cost forces us to cut corners and compromise. Jesus knew this, adding, "Any of you who does not renounce all that he has cannot be my disciple."[5]

Wow, Jesus. Really? Do You mean that? Can't You cut us a little slack? Can't we just ease into this discipleship thing?

Was the Lord saying, "You can't own anything"? No, but He is saying that nothing can own you. We can't serve two masters. If anything owns our loyalty or affections more than Christ, then that loyalty is misplaced. And for the disciple, misplaced loyalty is a sure way to ruin our witness in this world.

Jesus the Christ is asking, even demanding to be our exclusive Master. The question is, does He deserve this or not?

> Jesus the Christ is asking, even demanding to be our exclusive Master.

Counting the cost means you may be asked to sacrifice much for your Lord. I'm sure there were times the disciples thought, *Whoa, this isn't what I signed up for.* I fear many are saying the same thing today. And why? They've been misled by false teachers who promise all gain and no loss. They seek to make God our servant instead of making servants of God. This "name it and claim it" pseudo-gospel works well at home, but try it in Rwanda. Consumerism is a counterfeit gospel.

God doesn't exist for our benefit. We exist for His glory! Jesus frees us from slavery to materialism. He frees us to live beyond the pursuit of things. His call is to live for something greater.

Banking on the Gospel or Bankruptcy?

Ours is a culture of extremes. And sadly the church is no

different. It's the prosperity gospel versus the poverty gospel. Those in the prosperity-gospel camp shout, "If you just had enough faith, you'd be a millionaire. Sow financial seed and you'll reap financial prosperity." To them God is a celestial slot machine. Drop a few bucks in the machine and, like magic, you're wealthy. But like all other get-rich-quick schemes, you never hear about the millions of people for whom it didn't work.

Does extreme self-denial somehow make a person more spiritual and closer to God?

On the other end of the extreme, the poverty-gospel camp says, "If you had enough faith, you'd give away all your stuff and trust God to take care of you. Material things are unnecessary and even unspiritual." There's a temptation to a form of asceticism, or the idea that extreme self-denial somehow makes a person more spiritual and closer to God. This poverty gospel is now being tagged "the new legalism."

So which is right? The poverty gospel or the prosperity gospel?

Actually, neither. The Bible teaches instead a personal gospel, or doing what Christ has personally asked of you. Many people in Scripture had great wealth (Job, Abraham, Solomon, David) while others didn't (Lazarus,[6] the disciples, Jesus). Peter informed a homeless beggar, "I have no silver and gold, but what I do have I give to you. In the name of Jesus Christ of Nazareth, rise up and walk!"[7] Jesus told a wealthy scribe who desired to follow Him, "Foxes have holes, and birds of the air have nests, but the Son of Man has nowhere to lay his head."[8]

In our world, there are the haves and the have-nots. Wealth becomes a problem when it's a primary pursuit and drives our life. Poverty is a problem when we spend our life consumed by greed and envy of others. Jesus isn't against us having money as long as it's under His control, nor is He interested in us being consumed by greed and envy of others. Fifth-Gospel Christians know if God owns their bank account, checkbook, and credit cards, then there's a very good chance He also owns their heart.[9]

However, this requirement of discipleship is often the straw that breaks the camel's back. It can be the deal-breaker, as it was when Jesus encountered a rich young ruler.[10] Someone has wisely said, "Money is a great servant but a cruel master."

Following Jesus Will Mean Letting Go of False Beliefs

I once heard a story about a Hindu who became a Christian at a church service. Following his powerful experience, he went up to the preacher and said, "This is so great. I've become a Christian. Now I have Jesus, Krishna, Buddha, and Shiva."

Oops. We don't add Jesus to an existing all-star lineup of gods, as if we're collecting supernatural action figures. Following Christ means He alone reigns exclusively in our lives.

Following Christ means He alone reigns exclusively in our lives.

Simon the magician wanted a relationship with Christ, not because he loved Jesus but because he saw Christianity as a means to build on his magical talents. He even tried to purchase a little magical power. Obviously, this didn't rest well with Peter, who sternly rebuked him.[11] Simon had some false beliefs he needed to kiss goodbye.

Following Jesus May Cost Your Reputation

Many people try to fit in and enhance their reputation in the world. Since exposing their faith in Jesus may threaten their social standing, they attempt to live under the radar as "secret service" Christians. They travel incognito, preserving their status while trading in their faith.

But when a person becomes a follower of Jesus, His reputation becomes their primary focus. We are given a new reputation and new identity. Paul wrote, "Therefore, if anyone is in Christ, he is a new creation. The old has passed away; behold, the new has come."[12] Christ gives us this new sense of who we are. A fresh start!

Fifth-Gospel Christians learn how to walk according to their new identity. And people take notice. But some of these changes may cost you friendships. Are you prepared for that? Are you ready for the impact a total allegiance to Jesus may have on your friends, classmates, coworkers, and family?

Following Jesus May Cost You Your Job

Christ doesn't call everyone of His followers into full-time vocational ministry, but He does call some. Ever since He walked the earth, He has been calling people away from their careers and sending them into the mission fields to spread the Gospel. We all have to ask ourselves, "If Christ called me away from my current employment, would I follow? No matter what the call? Even to the mission field?"

Relieved He hasn't called you to Bangladesh, you are nevertheless His missionary at work. Following Christ may cost you in your job as you refuse to compromise your convictions in the area of ethics or morality (lying about financial reports, misleading customers). Or your allegiance to Christ might simply make life occasionally uncomfortable for you in a sometimes hostile environment. Are you willing to pay this price? To live with this tension?

Following Jesus May Cost You Your Freedom

Every since the church began, persecution has been prevalent. In His Sermon on the Mount, Jesus said, "Blessed are those who are persecuted for righteousness' sake, for theirs is the kingdom of heaven."[13] If you live a Fifth-Gospel life, there is no guarantee that people are going to be drawn to you. Paul writes, "For we are the aroma of Christ to God among those who are being saved and among those who are perishing, to one a fragrance from death to death, to the other a fragrance from life to life."[14] In the New Testament, many unbelievers were saved through observing Fifth-Gospel Christians, while many were martyred for those same beliefs and commitment.

As you can see, following Jesus can be costly. Risky. Daring. Dangerous. A true adventure. Always has been. There's no guarantee of safety, popularity, power, privilege, or success. As we move closer toward the return of Christ, things are likely to heat up for us. Therefore, our love for God must be extravagant and wholehearted, without compromise.

Following Jesus May Cost You Your Comfort

Thomas à Kempis, a fifteenth-century devotional writer, once wrote,

> Jesus has many who love his kingdom in heaven, but few who bear his cross. He has many who desire comfort, but few who desire suffering. He finds many to share his feast, but few his fasting. All desire to rejoice with him, but few are willing to suffer for his sake. Many follow Jesus to the breaking of bread, but few to the drinking of the cup of his passion. Many admire his miracles, but few follow him in the humiliation of the cross.[15]

His words still ring true today and sting us with conviction.

During my time at Dallas Theological Seminary, I met a fellow student from India named Sam. Small in stature and dressed simply, he was a most unintimidating man. Sam had jet-black hair and dark eyes, and yet he had a white-hot passion for Christ. One day we were eating lunch together in the cafeteria when he said, "Bobby, I have prepared myself for a life of suffering. And I'm not suffering here in America." He had counted the cost, and he was troubled because life felt too comfortable here in America.

"Bobby, pray for my country," he said later. "They have just made it illegal to preach the Gospel there."

"Do you still plan to go back?" I said.

"But of course," he quickly replied.

Another man who left comfort to follow Christ is my friend Sid Antley. I invited Sid to help start the church where I serve as lead pastor, and after much prayer, Sid called to say, "We have decided to leave Louisiana to come help you start the church. I just ask that you pray for me because I'm quitting my job and emptying out my 401(k)." I was blown away by Sid's huge step of faith as he and his family moved to North Carolina to help us start the church.

Following God is rarely safe, but we can rest assured that He is good.

In C.S. Lewis's most famous Narnia chronicle, *The Lion, the Witch, and the Wardrobe,* Lucy wondered if Aslan, the great lion, was safe. Mr. Beaver replied, "Safe? Who said anything about safe? Course he isn't safe. But he's good. He's the King, I tell you." A survey of the Scriptures and church history reveals that wholeheartedly following God is rarely safe, but we can rest assured that He is good. Unfortunately, there are no seat belts and no air bags to the spiritual life. The price we pay may be great, but it's worth it.

John Bunyan wrote *Pilgrims Progress* from prison. Put there for preaching the Gospel, Bunyan's allegory tells the story about Christian's pilgrimage to heaven. It's an adventure-filled and perilous journey, but in the end he arrives safely at the Celestial City. You are that pilgrim. His journey is yours. Though neither safe nor easy, we are assured God will bring us home.

Following Jesus May Cost You Your Dreams

Everybody has aspirations for their life. We all have an idea of how we hope things will turn out. Part of counting the cost is realizing that, along the way, our plans may not turn out to be His plans. Being a disciple of Jesus involves resigning ourselves to the fact that His ways are not our ways.[16] It means admitting that God may actually have a better idea than the one we've mapped out for our life's journey. This is something we must come to terms with.

It's only as we live God-aligned lives that true fulfillment is possible.

Of course, God may fulfill our dreams completely, or He may ask us to let go of them in exchange for His vision for our lives. The dreams of God must become our dreams.

It's only as we live God-aligned lives that true fulfillment is possible. And as we walk in His ways, we can best glorify God, bringing attention and honor to His name.

Following Jesus May Cost You Your Family

We typically think of losing our family because of our faith in the context of converting from another faith (like Islam) to Christianity. But a more realistic scenario in America is the potential ridicule or misunderstanding encountered when a believer really begins living their faith. This happens when you limit your children's TV, movie, or gaming habits. When you say no to that sleepover or prom date. It happens when your church takes a stand on a controversial social or moral issue, and your parents or siblings don't get it. It happens when your commitment to your community of faith conflicts with extended family plans. Unbelievers don't always understand why we do the things we do and why we embrace certain values. We can't expect them to.[17] We simply count the cost and keep loving them.

Sometimes new believers trust Christ and expect their families to be elated, only to meet resistance. They leave a church gathering after surrendering their lives to Jesus and think, *I can't wait to tell Mom and Dad.* And guess what? Mom and Dad aren't always interested. In fact, their new faith may lead to family rejection. In an increasingly post-Christian, pluralistic culture, we can expect more and more of this to occur. Jesus predicted this and reminded us in light of it to count the cost.[18]

Ultimately, Following Jesus May Even Cost You Your Life

Jesus' followers have paid a costly price over the past two thousand years, beginning with the apostles and the early church. Simply read the book of Acts to get a taste of what these Christians endured for their faith. And tradition tells us that most, if not all, of the apostles were martyred, though we can't be certain of the specifics.

What we do know is that these apostles took the words of Jesus seriously. They followed in His footsteps, sometimes shedding their blood in bold belief. Their life was Fifth-Gospel caliber! In his letter to the Philippians, Paul explained his motivation for enduring such suffering: "that I may known him and the power of his resurrection, and may share his sufferings, becoming like him in his death."[19]

Counting the cost for Christ in the midst of persecution produces boldness in other believers.

Their faith was so solid that they not only saw martyrdom as a possibility for their witness, but a hope. They figured, "We're all going to die somehow, what better way to die than to die for Jesus?" Counting the cost for Christ in the midst of persecution produces boldness in other believers, and in turn, God can use our witness to help foster faith in the hearts of the lost.

The apostles remembered Jesus' famous words from His Sermon on the Mount, "Blessed are you when others revile you and persecute you and utter all kinds of evil against you falsely on my account. Rejoice and be glad, for your reward is great in heaven, for so they persecuted the prophets who were before you."[20]

There's a reward for the persecuted, according to Jesus. And interestingly enough, right after He discusses the hardship and reward of persecution, Jesus shifts to being the salt of the earth and the light of the world:

> "You are the salt of the earth…You are the light of the world. A city set on a hill cannot be hidden. Nor do people light a lamp and put it under a basket, but on a stand, and it gives light to all in the house. In the same way, let your light shine before others, so that they may see your good works and give glory to your Father who is in heaven."[21]

The disciples knew that their lives never gave a greater witness for Christ than when they were being salt and light in the midst of persecution. They counted the cost.

Today, it's estimated that each year some 200,000 believers are killed for their faith in Jesus. That's 16,666 per month, nearly 548 every day. Many more die unknown, forgotten, and unreported. Their deaths are known only to God.

Is following Jesus worth losing your head to the jagged edge of a Muslim knife or a slow death in a Chinese or North Korean prison cell? Could there be a similar scenario coming closer to home at some point in the near future?

Fifth-Gospel Christians are willing to give up their wealth, lose their friends, face rejection, suffer persecution, and even die if necessary. All others who seek an easy life may achieve the American Dream, but they'll never realize the great adventure Christ has called them to.

All who seek an easy life may achieve the American Dream, but they'll never realize the great adventure Christ has called them to.

If we're honest, we have unspoken questions burning in our hearts: *Is this cost really worth it? Are there any benefits this side of eternity? Man, the cost seems too high.*

Whether the cost seems too high depends on our view of Jesus. Is He the Lamb who is worthy "to receive power and wealth and wisdom and might and honor and glory and blessing" as all heaven believes, or not?[22] You have to decide for yourself.

And it's not about works. It's about grace that changes us from the inside out. Grace works, and the world notices a life marked by it. The change within us is not motivated by a desire to prove ourselves to God or to be accepted by Him. Rather, the natural outcome of a life transformed by grace is a desire to live for Him because we have already been received by Him through Jesus.

Count the cost, Christian. And live boldly for the One who is worthy!

Loving Jesus and knowing Him far outweighs any price we may pay for being His disciple. It's the price we pay for the privilege of honoring our Lord and showing the world what a real Christian is. In fact, it was Jesus' love for us that caused Him to count the cost. If our lives are to bear the trademarks of discipleship, we must count the cost. We must reject the thinking that says, "Accept Jesus and live how you want." That Gospel never changed anyone or made a difference in the world. That doesn't produce a Fifth Gospel, but a false one. Though grace is free, it wasn't cheap. Count the cost, Christian. And live boldly for the One who is worthy!

In John 6, Jesus laid out the high cost of following Him. After hearing His words, many of His disciples walked away. Jesus then turned and looked at the Twelve and said, "Do you want to go away as well?" Peter said, "Lord, to whom shall we go? You have the words of eternal life."[23] Peter and the others had counted the cost.

Jesus is asking you the same question right now.

What are you going to say to Him?

GOSPEL APPEALS

- *The world won't see Christ living through you until you first die to the world.*
- *Grace may be free, but it wasn't cheap—it cost Jesus His life. What's it costing you?*
- *God doesn't exist for our benefit. We exist for His glory.*

Questions for Further Thought and Discussion

1. Let's face it. The cost is high for following Jesus. Does it seem like He was a bit irrational? I mean, can't we tailor things a bit for our progressive culture?

2. Do you think the church at large is really calling Christians to count the cost *or* are we offering a love-boat Christianity that's filled with all grace and no repentance?

3. What will be the consequences in our world if the church fails to count the cost?

4. Why do you think it's so hard to die to our own lives?

5. Can you describe a time when you were rejected for your faith?

6. If Jesus were to personally speak to you right now, what is the one thing He'd ask you to surrender to Him? Are you willing to do so?

Chapter 4

IDOL FACTORIES

"Little children,
keep yourselves from idols."

JOHN THE APOSTLE

For over one hundred years, the place where I live has been famous for manufacturing. From fabric to furniture, you can find plants and factories scattered all over the Carolinas. Cotton mills, car plants, and carpet manufacturers are all a part of our landscape, with some companies employing a high percentage of some small towns' populations. Some families have long histories of generations who worked the third shift in a textile mill, and it was assumed that successive generations would follow in their footsteps. And many have.

But for a few moments I'd like for us to imagine another kind of factory. This one isn't nestled into a mountain valley or sprawled out on some vast plain. It's not made of brick and mortar or wood and steel. This manufacturing plant doesn't churn out cotton or wooden bed frames. Instead, this factory produces a unique commodity, something so popular that it's doubtful it will ever go out of style. And though the supply is abundant, the demand remains strong.

Idol factories. They're everywhere. In every heart. In every person. In you. In me.

Idols of the Heart

We don't think very much about idols in our culture. After all, physical representations of deities are reserved for third-world countries. You find them in primitive cultures that have yet to evolve to our level of reason and scientific knowledge. Besides, we're way beyond bowing down to some sculpted object of wood, stone, gold, or silver. We're above stooping in submission to some culturally revered statue or symbol.

Aren't we?

Or is it possible that we have merely sophisticated the traditional knee-bend, transforming it into something a bit more, shall we say, dignified?

To fully answer this question, and to understand exactly how these heart-idols impact our witness for Christ, we have to first understand what they are. When Moses descended Mount Sinai after receiving the Ten Commandments from God, he encountered a different people than he had left forty days earlier. While their leader was away, the people had petitioned Moses's brother Aaron to "make us gods who shall go before us."[1] They had grown tired of waiting for God's man to come down from that mountain. They weren't satisfied with the invisible God they had and demanded something a little more tangible.

So, out of his own mind, Aaron melted down all the gold they had taken from Egypt and from it fashioned an image of a golden calf. This shiny, expensive object became the focus of the people's allegiance, energy, and worship. They partied around it, even building an altar before it. And it didn't take long for their celebration to devolve into a gluttonous feast and drunken orgy.[2]

It was Mardi Gras at Mount Sinai.

Recognizing Our Golden Calves

But wait a minute. We're not all like those primitive desert-walkers. I mean, when was the last time you melted down your gold jewelry, made a cow out of it, and threw a party to worship it? I'm thinking maybe…never? We don't see statues of Molech or Baal at the mall entrance or fixed atop the local baseball field. We're not that backward or barbaric. But are there any modern-day equivalents of these ancient idols? And if so, then how do we recognize these unseen golden calves?

First, let's define the concept. Idols are a representation of what we honor, esteem, pay allegiance to, or worship. They're the things we live for apart from God—the things that motivate us. They're what we desire above all else, *the God-replacements* we use to give us the things we want and need—significance, happiness, and a feeling of worth.

Idols are the things we're convinced we cannot be happy without.

Idols tell us we have a place in the world. That we belong. That we matter. They're the things we're convinced we cannot be happy without. These idols demand our time, effort, energy, and resources. They captivate our hearts, demanding our attention and even our worship. And though they may not speak, we nevertheless hear their voices calling to us above the white noise that surrounds us. We even hear their voices coming from our own hearts.

You may find it difficult to envision yourself as an idol worshipper. I do. I read about those calf worshippers at Sinai and think, *Those people are wacko! I could never do that.*

But could it be that we are just as blinded, but by a more sophisticated form of idolatry? Could it be that it's now much more difficult to detect idolatry because it's more stylish, tame, and erudite than the animal worshippers of Exodus? Is it possible that we've purchased membership into the idol club without even realizing it?

Idolatry Is Alive and Well

If we're honest, we have to admit to struggling with idolatry. Same golden calf, just packaged differently. Same product, different label. It's Idolatry 2.0, the updated version. Call it neo-idolatry, but today idolatry is more alive than ever. Right here in America. In your community. In your church. Idolatry is not some relic of the past, but rather a present, dark reality. And our hearts are idol factories.

While on a trip to eastern India, an American pastor describes walking down a dirt road and coming upon a shrine where they were sacrificing chickens. Blood and feathers were everywhere. He says there are idols as far as the eye can see and the Indians worship everything you can possibly imagine. When he asked one of the women there if she would ever visit the United States, she said, "I did once and I will never come again. I cannot stomach the idolatry."

This was the last thing the pastor expected to hear as he watched chickens being sacrificed on an altar. So he asked the woman, "Where do you see the shrines of false worship and idolatry in our culture?" She said, "Your god is your stomach with your restaurants everywhere. Your god is your sports teams and you build multimillion-dollar stadiums to house them. Your god is your television and all the chairs in your home are lined up so that your family can gather around the altar and worship that god."[3]

Idolatry is a human problem. And none of us is above it.

Regardless of the forms it takes, idolatry is not an Indian or American problem. It's a human problem. And none of us is above it. Perhaps the famed atheist Friedrich Nietzsche was on to something when he said, "There are more idols in the world than there are realities."[4]

Ten Nonnegotiables

So let's dig a little deeper into the nature of idolatry. At its core, an idol is a God-supplanter. It's anything in our life that we love more than we love Him. Call them God substitutes, filling our hearts, affections, and minds with created things rather than the Creator.

But back to Moses for a minute. While he was on top of Mount Sinai, God Himself handchiseled ten nonnegotiables into stone for His people. He intended these requirements to guide Israel and keep them aligned vertically and horizontally. They weren't ultra-lofty moral standards meant for the spiritually elite, but rather elementary standards for how Israel was to relate to God and to their fellow humans. Have you ever thought about their meaning in contemporary language? Perhaps we could paraphrase them this way:

1. Because I am the only true God, don't put anything ahead of Me in your life. This is really a no-brainer.
2. Don't bow down to a piece of wood, stone, silver, or gold. Do I have to explain how dumb that makes you look?
3. Don't be flippant or shallow when you talk about Me.
4. Take a day of rest each week. It's good for you.
5. Honor your parents. They know more about life than you do.
6. Don't murder other people.
7. Don't have sex with anyone other than your spouse.
8. Don't steal other people's stuff or what doesn't belong to you.
9. Don't tell lies to each other.
10. Don't burn with desire for what other people have.

That pretty much covers the basic areas of life, both broad and specific. These ten standards were given by God to provide a full and meaningful life for His people and to protect them from despair, pain, and heartache. And keeping the first one is the key to keeping the other nine. Unfortunately, we have trouble keeping number one.

"You shall have no other gods before me."[5] How simple, right? Just don't put anything ahead of God. Nothing. Nada. Besides, what other deities actually exist? None, of course. And yet we still manufacture them in assembly-line fashion in that heart-shaped idol factory of ours. It's because of this that God commands us to shut that factory down. Close up shop.

> Often an idol is simply an abuse of a good thing, making a good thing a "first thing."

And notice the phrase "no other gods before me." It's not that we can't enjoy other things, but those "other things" are secondary things, less important things. Often an idol is simply an abuse of a good thing, making a good thing a "first thing." But God must be first in everything we do.

In 1951, C.S. Lewis wrote in a letter, "Put first things first and we get second things thrown in: put second things first and we lose *both* first and second things."[6] Lewis was echoing Jesus' words from His Sermon on the Mount: "But seek first the kingdom of God and his righteousness, and all these things will be added to you."[7] All what things? Second things. Other good and necessary things. But this can happen only when God's righteousness is of first importance. And why? Because His righteousness, essence, and holiness is the "greatest good."

We waste much of life chasing secondary things. When other things consume us and become our ultimate, we dramatically shrink our Fifth-Gospel witness. The world and the flesh seek pleasure in second things. But Christ-followers distinguish themselves by keeping God in His rightful place…first in everything.

The problem with idols is they become the center of our lives. In his *New York Times* best seller, *The Reason for God*, Timothy Keller writes:

If you center your life and identity on your spouse or partner, you will be emotionally dependent, jealous, and controlling.

If you center your life and identity on your family and children, you will try to live your life through your children until they resent you or have no self of their own.

If you center your life and identity on your work and career, you will be a driven workaholic and a boring, shallow person.

If you center your life and identity on money and possessions, you'll be eaten up by worry or jealousy about money.

If you center your life and identity on pleasure, gratification, and comfort, you will find yourself getting addicted to something.

If you center your life and identity on relationships and approval, you will be constantly overly hurt by criticism and thus always losing friends.

If you center your life and identity on a "noble cause," you will divide the world into "good" and "bad" and demonize your opponents.

If you center your life and identity on religion and morality, you will, if you are living up to your moral standards, be proud, self-righteous, and cruel. If you don't live up to your moral standards, your guilt will be utterly devastating.[8]

All good things. But not worthy of first place in our lives.

American Idols

So what do some of our contemporary idols look like? How would we recognize these criminal cravings? Can you pick them out of a lineup? See if the following look familiar.

Idol 1: Stuff (Matthew 6:19-21)

Ours is perhaps the most materialistic society in the history of planet Earth. We are obsessed with accumulating and having things. Cars. Homes. Boats. Motorcycles. Pools. Giant TVs. Closets full of clothes. Pantries stocked with food. You name it and we either have it or are working on getting it. And while having possessions isn't at all wrong, it can easily get out of hand and become the tail that wags the dog. Take some time to look around your home and ask yourself, *Do I really need all this stuff? If God asked me to let it go, could I?*

Idol 2: Cash (Matthew 6:24)

In a struggling economy, everyone everywhere scrambles to get all the assets they can and then guard them with their lives. As consumer prices rise, so rises the desperate search for ways to make more money. But even in good times, there never seems to be enough, does there? It's the idol factory within us that whispers "Just a little bit more!"

Idol 3: Sex (Job 31:1; Ephesians 5:3; 2 Timothy 2:22)

Sexual pleasure is a narcotic more toxic and addictive than any drug. Tens of millions are enslaved to pornography and a fantasy world of sexual experience and fulfillment. Advertisements, art, media, movies, and the Internet have all contributed to our seemingly insatiable craving for this natural human drug of choice. Again, a good thing when celebrated in marriage, but outside of that context, an idol that subtly, and sometimes not so subtly, creeps up on us.

Idol 4: Technology

Our culture is driven by technology. It's our society's life-support machine. Try living without it for a day or two and your friends may think of you as a caveman holding some primitive stone weapon. Technology is the highway upon which our lives, business, and communication travel. It's here to stay, and is constantly advancing to meet society's changing demands. As believers we balance ourselves on the tightrope between technology as tool and technology as master and time-stealer. Just for fun, try not checking your phone, Facebook, or Twitter for a whole day and see how you feel. You'll soon discover just how important it is to you and how dependent you are on it.

Idol 5: Beauty (Proverbs 31:30; 1 Peter 3:3-4)

We are obsessed with appearance, evident by a multibillion dollar industry dedicated to making us look better and younger. Botox, implants, cosmetics, expensive skin creams, tanning beds, hair coloring, hair replacement, liposuction—there is seemingly no end to the vain pursuit of beauty. And once again, it's not a sin to want to look your best or to wear makeup. But wisdom and spirituality suggest an invisible line exists between looking good and bowing down to the idol of society's idea of beauty. You can have so many face-lifts that when you smile your toes curl up! They don't call it a "vanity mirror" for no reason. Make the beauty of character a greater value than outward appearance, and the latter will take care of itself.

Idol 6: Entertainment

America is the entertainment capital of the world. Hollywood, college and professional sports, hunting, video gaming, big-arena concerts are all a part of our country's collective amusement. It's estimated that the average American spends five hours a day watching television.[9] Young people now spend more time on their phones texting, playing games, listening to music, and watching videos than they do talking on them.[10] This doesn't even take into account the time young people spend in online gaming. Seven out of ten kids have a TV in their bedroom. Are we raising a generation of media junkies? How will they get their fix in ten years? Can our young people initiate and engage in rational thought without being entertained? Is this why children and youth ministers are having such a difficult time attracting kids to church?

Idol 7: Success

The pressure to achieve is greater than ever before. In a highly competitive marketplace, it's dog-eat-dog, with the bigger, stronger canine usually prevailing. Small businesses and entrepreneurs are forced to shut down or even declare bankruptcy due to a failure to succeed against the competition. Of course, the pursuit of excellence is a good and noble thing, but like anything else, it can stealthfully turn on you, demanding your highest allegiance. On the treacherous road to success, it becomes easy to cast aside the things that once guided you in order to fast-track your way to the top. Little white lies and ethical compromise all contribute to cutting corners and looking for shortcuts to the winner's circle. And this isn't just found in secular society. In an effort to appear more successful, pastors have also been known to pad membership and financial numbers to impress their peers in subtle competition.

Idol 8: Religion

Perhaps the most covert idol of all is religion, specifically the Christian faith. But how could that be? Isn't our faith supposed to be the most important thing in our lives? Well, sorta. A spiritually minded person has to develop the sensitivity to know when Christian values and activities are replacing Christ, to discern when godly things become more important than God Himself. As followers of Jesus, we can unknowingly worship the Christian faith instead of the Christ. We prioritize biblical principles over the Person of God.

We have more allegiance to our church than to the One we claim to worship. We love Bible studies more than God. It's like being in love with the idea of love instead of being in love with the person we claim to love!

We don't need more Christian stuff. We need more people whose passion is the Person of Christ.

If you see yourself as a "religious" person, it's time to reevaluate. If being with your Christian friends, being in a Bible study, being a member of a church, singing or playing in a worship band, or being a spiritual leader mean more to you than Jesus does, you have an idol problem.

We don't need more Christian stuff. We need more people whose passion is the Person of Christ.

None of these are anything new, of course. Centuries ago, Solomon earned a PhD in idol making. With the brains and bucks to pull it off, he pursued life's pleasures to the max, concluding they were all a giant, collective *zero*.[11] He concluded that, until the pursuit of God enters the equation, the rest of life's experiences are worth nothing.[12] A waste of breath, energy, and time.

In his book *Seeing with New Eyes*, David Powlison has a chapter titled "X-Ray Questions." In it are thirty-five heart-probing questions designed to detect one's functional gods, the idols that lurk within our hearts. Uncovering those hidden idols requires blunt self-disclosure and honesty. To help you identify what idols may be creeping up on you, I encourage you to go to www.acts29network .org/acts-29-blog/x-ray-questions/ and prayerfully go through these questions as a means of spotting potential idols.

Paul wrote to the Corinthians, "Therefore, if anyone is in Christ, he is a new creation. The old has passed away; behold, the new has come."[13] One reason so many Christians struggle to experience life change is that they still feel the old zombie living in them. They forget that they're a new creation in Christ. That's why those old idols, those old gods, feel so real and comfortable. Yet in reality, they're dead to us. We can't effectively deal with our idolatry until we first realize we are a new creation. If we could truly understand who we are in Christ, our lives would be radically different. The good news is that we can crush the idols of our heart. But like life itself, it is a daily thing.

"Filth Gospel" Versus the Fifth Gospel

Replacing God with another ultimate pursuit causes us to shrink our witness. The world is waiting to see a church that loves and worships and adores and praises and makes much of God. As

Augustine exhorted, "Our loves must be rightly ordered." God must become our highest pursuit in our everyday choices. The secret to crushing the idols of our heart is to crave God. When He becomes our greatest and deepest desire, all other things will pale in comparison. C.S. Lewis said, "We are half-hearted creatures, fooling about with drink and sex and ambition when infinite joy is offered us, like an ignorant child who wants to go on making mud pies in a slum because he cannot imagine what is meant by the offer of a holiday at the sea. We are far too easily pleased."[14]

And therein lies the problem.

The reason we chase idols and crown them king in our hearts is because we find more joy in them than we do in God. They seem real and they give us something. Some pleasure. Some satisfaction. A sense of self-importance or self-exaltation. Euphoria. Happiness. Security. The very things God Himself desires to give us.

But because of our magnetic attraction to these idols, we are pulled in, drawn to them like a moth to a flame. Or maybe like an addict to the next fix. Before long we are permanently tethered to them. They become our umbilical cord, our lifeline to substance, sustenance, and life itself. They become the epicenter of who we are, and we are—either partially or entirely—defined by them. God is pushed to the periphery. Marginalized, He becomes second-string (or third), and we call upon Him only when our first-string lets us down or fails to perform. Instead of being our life-support, God becomes more like dialing 9-1-1…only in case of emergency. Oh, we may still display a respectable godly exterior, but the core of our being is energized and motivated by another god altogether.

How ridiculous would it look to see people in your local park dancing half-naked around a golden calf? But it didn't look ridiculous to the Israelites because everyone was doing it. They experienced peer pressure—worship style. But it also fit their time and culture. Imagine how silly it looks from heaven's perspective when we dance around our American idols.

Israel was chastised and disciplined by the Lord for worshipping gods who were silent statues. "You have gods but they cannot speak."[15] But ah, our modern idol-gods do speak. They give us important information. They carry us from one place to another. They make us feel good. They make us smarter. They give us purpose and direction. They give us a reason to get up in the morning. They entertain us. Make us laugh. Motivate us. We can actually see our idols. But God we cannot see. Inherently addicted to our physical senses and emotionally incomplete, we settle for just about anything that will give us what we need to feel loved, wanted, and important.

> We settle for just about anything that will give us what we need to feel loved, wanted, and important.

This is a tragedy of the greatest magnitude. We have to learn how to find our ultimate joy in God alone. (Hang in there for the next chapter, where we will explore this idea in more detail.)

Game of Thrones

One of the greatest ways idol worship harms us (other than the obvious attempt to dethrone God in our lives) is that it damages our ability to reflect Jesus Christ to a watching world. It creates confusion because people are left wondering where our allegiance really lies. It causes us to blend in rather than stand out and be distinctive. It morphs our identity into one of those nameless dancing Israelites.

Another problem with idols is we tend to become like the things we worship. When something becomes your god, your character eventually molds to it. Your mind adapts to it. Your actions and lifestyle reflect it. In contrast, consider David's journal thoughts:

> As the deer pants for streams of water,
>   so my soul pants for you, my God.[16]

Have you ever panted for God? Felt your lips crack and your

throat go dry longing for Him? Ever been desperately dependent on Him, so much so that you forgot every other important thing in your life? This kind of longing isn't given to a chair-warming churchgoer. It's not available to conservative-thinking citizens. It's not awarded to Christians too busy with the things of God to encounter God Himself.

It's experienced only by those who see their life's pursuits for what they really are…empty and meaningless. It comes to those who see Yahweh as their ultimate and only hope. Their one great love. Their consuming passion. Their burning desire.

Confess Jesus as your ultimate pursuit, and then you will become all you're meant to be.

When this becomes true of us, we reflect His image instead of other images. Jesus Christ is the image of God and the exact representation of His being.[17] Acknowledge and confess Him as your ultimate pursuit, and then you will become all you're meant to be. Then, and only then, will the world see the real Gospel of Jesus Christ.

So what altars do you need to tear down? Do you need to have a funeral or two for some of your gods? To bury those graven images in a grave. If so, I trust this chapter has firmly placed a shovel in your hands.

I urge you to start digging.

GOSPEL APPEALS

- *Idolatry is not something from the past. It's a present reality that's more alive than ever before.*

- *Idolatry is the sin of creating pseudo-ultimates in place of the ultimate Ultimate.*

- *When Christ is your Ultimate, He looks magnificent through your life.*

Questions for Further Thought and Discussion

1. Why do you think it's so hard for us in today's culture to think of ourselves as idol worshippers?

2. What are some modern equivalents to ancient idolatry, and why do you think it's so easy for each culture to be blinded by its own idols?

3. The famed atheist Friedrich Nietzsche said, "There are more idols in the world than there are realities." What do you think he was getting at, and do you agree or disagree?

4. Bobby mentioned several idols in this chapter. Can you think of any other idols that people commonly struggle with?

5. Can you think of an idol in your own life that needs to be dealt with?

6. Do you think it's true that we become like the things we focus on? If that's the case, why do you think it is so critical to spend solid time pondering the God we love?

Chapter 5

CONTAGIOUS JOY

"God is most glorified in you when you are most satisfied in Him."

JOHN PIPER

God is so awesome…and at the same time, so seemingly random.

Case in point. While on a trip to Jerusalem in 2013, I met a man named Noam in the lobby of the Leonardo Hotel. Noam grew up like most Israelis with a strong Jewish foundation. Following high school, he served in the army as a tank commander during the first Lebanon war. As we talked, Noam told me he'd left Israel to study martial arts in Japan. He devoted himself to the art of Ninja in a search for meaning in life. After twenty-one years, he returned to Israel.

One day, while working in a jewelry store in Qumran, he met Deborah. Deborah was so filled with a God-centered joy that she and her friends began dancing right there in the jewelry store. Watching this unusual display

We should never underestimate the power of joy before a lost and dying world.

of joy, Noam realized that something was still missing in his life. God used the simple yet extravagant joy of Deborah to point Noam to Jesus. Today he is not only a sold-out Fifth-Gospel Christian, he's also Deborah's husband! He was doubly blessed that day, meeting his Savior and his bride. We should never underestimate the power of joy before a lost and dying world.

So what's the deal with joy? I'm not talking about a personality trait or natural temperament. I'm not referring to that gal with the bubbly personality or the man with the perpetually positive attitude. Being joyful has very little to do with skipping down life's road whistling "Zip-a-Dee-Doo-Dah." And it has nothing to do with that glassy-eyed church member with the ever-present, praise-the-Lord smile on her face. That's a little creepy.

But there does exist a joy that actually creates a curious thirst in others. It's a contagious attitude that makes people want what you have. It builds bridges and creates a relationship platform through which to share the hope that is within you.[1]

I believe the church should be the most joyful place in the world. We are the ones whose sins have been forgiven, who've been redeemed and been given a confident hope and future. We know God and are heaven bound. Hey, salvation is a pretty good deal. Yet sadly, for many of us, our faces contradict the joy we claim our hearts possess.

> I've never seen a miserable-looking person and thought, *I wish I could have some of what he's got.*

One of the missing links to effective evangelism today is a lack of joy. We can defend our faith until we're blue in the face, but if we don't have joy, our message won't be compelling. I've never seen a miserable-looking person and thought, *I wish I could have some of what he's got.*

But joyful people are infectious. Joy is one of the Christian's secret weapons. It demonstrates that our faith is tangible and real. Joy brings credibility. It even makes what we have *desirable*. Joy is the default emotional state of one who has grasped the depth of the

Gospel. It's the state of a person who knows he's rightly related to God. And people can't help but notice.

The Command to Be Joyful

So how does someone get this joy? Believe it or not, Christians are actually commanded to be joyful. *Joy* and *rejoice* radiate throughout Paul's letter to the Philippians, and he concludes by exhorting them to "Rejoice in the Lord always; again I will say, rejoice."[2] Really, Paul? Joyful? Always? Is this humanly possible?

First, does it surprise you that Paul actually *commands us to be joyful*? He uses a Greek word *chairō* ("rejoice") to help us understand this commandment more clearly. Paul is not talking about *happiness*. Happiness has to do with what's happening to us, while joy is grounded in God, His Word, what He has done for us, and our anticipation of Christ's glorious return.

Happiness is largely affected by our circumstances and is more emotional in nature. Joy is primarily a state of mind that influences those emotions. One is rooted in ever-changing circumstances and life situations while the other finds its source in God who never changes.

Isn't it amazing that we serve a God who desires our joy? What a refreshing picture of God, who is often accused of being "unfun." Far from it.

We serve a God who desires our joy.

How many nonbelievers do you know who have been disillusioned by joyless, overserious Christians? We can change that. But it begins with a transformed mind.[3] If God can transform the way we think, our joy will increase. And apparently attitude matters to God. Do you recall Israel in the wilderness, murmuring and complaining to God? As a result of this attitude, they were prohibited from going into the Promised Land. God didn't want to send a bunch of grumblers into His land of promise. They needed to be a contagious group, a set-apart group, a people God intended to be a light to the nations.[4]

Some scholars believe *chairō* also carries the idea of boasting with an exultant joy. The word then implies the notion of rejoicing *out loud*. You could say real joy has a *leak* to it.

Joy Begins and Ends with God

Second, God Himself is both *the source and the object of our joy*. As we find our enjoyment in God, we begin seeing Him in the middle of everything we do. It's living with a sense of "God consciousness." But notice specifically that Paul says, "Rejoice *in the Lord*." That's because the foundation and focus of our joy is God—not primarily circumstances or people. Our joy begins and ends with God, and that starts with Him being our greatest delight in life.

Let's be real. We all want joy, don't we? I mean, who wakes up and prays, *God, make me miserable today*? One reason so many are miserable is because they are seeking joy in things that are powerless to give them joy. That's like trying to squeeze orange juice from a cell phone. Not gonna happen. According to Scripture, God is where the joy is. David said,

> You make known to me the path of life;
> in your presence there is *fullness of joy*;
> at your right hand are *pleasures forevermore*.[5]

Fullness of joy? Pleasures? Forevermore? Wow. Is that what comes to your mind when you think about God? When you think about church? The Christian life? Obedience? Prayer? Worship? Do you associate *pleasure* with all those things? David is making a bold claim here. He's saying that life lived in the presence of God brings the highest and most enjoyable experience known to humankind. He's saying that those who live in Him experience pleasure—a life satisfaction like nothing else.

> Life lived in the presence of God brings the most enjoyable experience known to humankind.

It's something better than entertainment. Better than seeing your team win the Super Bowl. Better than going on a shopping spree. Better than your dream vacation. Better than getting a huge bonus at work. Better than drugs. Better than sex. Seriously.

Could God really be *that* amazing? Could being connected with Him in relationship really be that great? Better than anything this life and world has to offer?

Do you believe that?

Finding our joy in the Lord helps recalibrate our minds. Our default perspective on life is skewed by sin and our fallen nature. But dwelling on Christ and what He has done for us reboots our thinking. It changes our attitude. It gives us a hope-filled vision for our lives and how we can interface with it. Joy even helps us cope with the uncertainties of daily life.

Obviously, we can find partial joy in some things and relationships, but they are subject to change every day. God, however, is the only reliable source to draw joy from. The source of our joy will determine the quantity and consistency of it. One of the reasons people create idols is that they think they will make them joyful. People want kids, houses, jobs, success, and friendships because they believe those things will add to their happiness. And much of it does. But God is the only constant where we can truly anchor our life.

> The source of our joy will determine the quantity and consistency of it.

Eight Is Enough

The Latin phrase *summum bonum* refers to the "greatest good, the final end or purpose in life." For centuries, philosophers and theologians such as Confucius, Buddha, Mohammad, Nietzsche, and many more have wrestled to identify the greatest good that one must pursue in order to achieve the greatest amount of happiness. Paul is claiming that God is that *summum bonum*, the greatest good and source of true happiness.[6] Anything that becomes our *summum bonum* becomes our god, and as we saw in the previous chapter, those things just don't cut it. But when our lives reveal God as the highest Good, then we have something worth exporting to a world that desperately needs hope and joy.

And yet people continue to search for that ultimate joy apart from God. Thomas Aquinas, the thirteenth-century medieval philosopher and theologian, gives us eight of the biggest pursuits.[7]

Wealth

Years ago, I was working as an intern at a church in Plano, Texas, and heard how their church offices had caught fire and burned to the ground several years before. While walking through the ash-filled ruins, the pastor had discovered in his office the only thing that survived the fire—a book he had written titled *Biblical Theology of Material Possessions*. Sometimes God has a sense of humor.

But it's no secret that in our culture, the pursuit of happiness involves attempting to travel the road to riches. But there is a reason Scripture warns to "keep your life free from *love* of money."[8]

Make no mistake about it, money can buy you a happy time or pleasurable experience, but it can't buy you love or ultimate joy. Money is merely a means to an end, not the end itself. People want money not for money's sake, but for what money can buy. Here is the impotence of wealth.

Unfortunately, some settle for the shallow happiness money can provide. But they never go deeper. As a result, they live lives of spiritual mediocrity, never knowing the depth or true richness of satisfaction God's joy can give. They miss out on real life, all the while under the illusion that they have it. And why? Because the world tells them to. They are sucked into the black hole of temporal values, blinded by greed, materialism, and the constant, insatiable desire for more. How tragic, sad, and unnecessary.

Even more sad are affluent Christians caught up in this mindset, continually accumulating wealth and things to make their lives more comfortable and envied by others. Is it any wonder Jesus told

His disciples, "For what will it profit a man if he gains the whole world and forfeits his soul?"[9]

Someone has said, "The problem with money is that money can buy only what money can buy." Money can't buy you eternal life, or forgiveness, or a perfect set of emotions, or an upgraded brain (though sometimes I wish it could).

> "The problem with money is that money can buy only what money can buy."

Interestingly, the countries with the highest suicide rate are those with the most wealth. John D. Rockefeller, once the richest man in the world and the first person to ever earn a billion dollars, was asked, "How much money is enough?" He responded, "Just a little bit more." Money can't give ultimate happiness.

Honor

You may have heard of "honor cultures" where the value of honor is highly esteemed. It is believed that with great honor comes true fulfillment and happiness. But no person can guarantee their own honor. Honor is something bestowed from another. As Peter Kreeft, professor of philosophy of religion at Boston College, writes, "Happiness can't consist in honor because happiness is in the person who is happy—it's internal. But honor comes from the person giving the honor and so is external."[10] Honor may add to one's happiness, but it can just as easily be stripped away. Again, this happiness is based on something that is unreliable and unpredictable. It's based on others' opinions of you. And though noble, honor falls short in supplying us with the joy we need.

Fame

We live in a culture where celebrity is king. Having fame means you're finally somebody. That you're genuinely important. That you matter. But fame can be a fickle friend, here today but gone tomorrow (when you're no longer the *flavor of the week*). Like honor, it's others who have the power to declare you famous or a has-been. It's a conditional state, like a great coach who is loved by millions of fans while he's winning, only to be tarred and feathered the moment his team falls from the winner's bracket.

Fame is, at best, a temporary buzz strapped into an emotional roller coaster. When the fame is alive and well, so is your happiness. But when the flame of your fame burns out and you end up in the "once famous" or "yesterday's news" file, you become a mere footnote, a relic in the celebrity museum. And there goes your joy.

Fame is an empty pursuit that can be experienced only by a select few.

Fame cannot be the *summum bonum* because it's something that can be experienced only by a select few. Not everyone can be famous. Fame is an empty pursuit. In contrast, we as Christians live for the fame of Another. *He* is the Famous One.

Power

Next in Aquinas's list is *power*. Of course, few of us will be heads of state or CEOs, but we are still lured by the tempting aroma of gaining power at work or over our friends or social circles. Some are more predisposed to this than others, but we still have to resist the desire to dominate others.

To be a Christian means to give up control, not gain it. Jesus said His followers would serve others, not rule over them.[11] The Gospel calls us to give our lives away. Power-seekers trample on others to ascend because the focus is self. It's the very opposite of a joy-filled, Fifth-Gospel life. Gaining power may give us authority over others, but real joy is found in giving life away, not in accumulating power.

Health

In the movie *Forever Young*, Mel Gibson plays a test pilot who volunteers for a cryogenics experiment in 1939. Fifty years later, he is thawed out and begins pursuing his long-lost love. Wouldn't it be great to freeze yourself to ensure that you'd have a healthy young body at forty-five, sixty, or eighty years old?

Health is a good thing, but here's an interesting statistic: one out of every one person dies. Good health can take us only so far, and then we age and pass on from this life. Time is ticking for all of us. Good health can provide some enjoyment and a certain quality of life, and as believers, we ought to care for our bodies. Botox, implants, hair color, liposuction, Lasik surgery, kale, wheatgrass, and flaxseed may help one feel and look younger, but eventually beauty and health fades. Therefore, health cannot be our *summum bonum*.

> Time is ticking for all of us.

Pleasure

Pleasure is a good thing. God created it and designed us to enjoy it. We find pleasure in any number of things, including entertainment, sex, art, travel, hobbies, sports, and music—all gifts from God. However, none of these can sustain happiness or joy for long. Just ask the wisest man who ever lived.[12]

We've all met people who were entertained yet empty inside. Neil Postman's book title *Amusing Ourselves to Death* accurately captures the American problem. When pleasure is the aim of our life, we are sure to eventually be disappointed and unfulfilled.

> The Christ-follower's joy transcends even pleasure. It goes higher and farther.

But the Christ-follower's joy transcends even pleasure. It goes higher and farther. Remember C.S. Lewis's assessment of our tendency to settle for lesser pleasures: "We are half-hearted creatures, fooling about with drink and sex and ambition when infinite joy is offered us, like an ignorant child who wants to go on making mud pies in a slum because he cannot imagine what is meant by the offer of a holiday at the sea. We are far too easily pleased."[13]

Easily pleased.

Bingo.

Virtue

Virtue is a noble and praiseworthy pursuit, right? And being morally upright and pure is a character quality valued in Scripture. We might agree that virtue will certainly lead to more happiness than chasing pleasure, honor, or health. But does it also have its limitations?

The Pharisees of Jesus' day prided themselves on being virtuous, but according to Christ, their virtue blinded them to their deepest need: "Woe to you, scribes and Pharisees, hypocrites! For you are like whitewashed tombs, which outwardly appear beautiful, but within are full of dead people's bones and all uncleanness. So you also outwardly appear righteous to others, but within you are full of hypocrisy and lawlessness."[14]

There is no real virtue apart from God. Jesus wanted them to know that virtue apart from God is relative, a sort of *pseudo-virtue*. Because we're made in God's image, true virtue points back to the Creator of that image. There is no real virtue apart from God. Scripture makes it crystal clear that we are far from being inherently virtuous.[15] Virtue is good, just not good enough to make us joyful.

God

After walking through these possible candidates for happiness, Aquinas concludes, "God alone constitutes man's happiness."[16] It stands to reason that no finite thing can grant ultimate happiness. No created thing can be our *summum bonum*. Paul put it this way, "For to me to live is Christ, and to die is gain."[17] Christ was his end because Christ was his God.

What about you? How would you fill in the following blanks?

"For to me to live is_____, and to die is _____."

What sums up life for you? What does it mean to really live? Your answer will reveal where you seek to find joy. Your answer reveals what you live for. Anything other than God Himself means death will rob you of your joy. And to die becomes loss for you. Only the

Christian can say, "For to me to live is *Christ*," and confidently proclaim, "to die is gain."

These words from Paul are found in the same letter where he says, "Rejoice in the Lord always; again I will say, rejoice."[18] He had every reason to rejoice because Jesus was his reason for living. Jesus was his Ultimate, his highest good and joy. As the psalmist wrote, "Joyful indeed are those whose God is the LORD."[19]

> Christians should be the world's greatest enthusiasts.

Can you now see more clearly why Christians should be the world's greatest enthusiasts? In fact, the word *enthusiasm* comes from two Greek words, *en* and *theos*—"in God." So the real enthusiast is the person who is "in God." Our salvation is our joy producer. And though they may not admit it, everyone wants this kind of joy. A joy that endures hard times and overcomes difficult seasons of life. A joy that protects us from imploding under the sometimes crushing weight of daily stress and problems. A joy that keeps us sane during a painful divorce, loss of a loved one, and disappointment. A joy that sustains us even when life doesn't go according to our plan or turn out like we expected.

> To the extent that our joy is found in Him, that joy becomes a witness.

Is that the kind of joy you have? Is that the kind of joy you desire?

We can lose our wealth, our honor, our fame, our power, our health, our pleasure, and even our virtue with a moral failure, but God is our constant. Steadfast. Unmovable. To the extent that our joy is found in Him, that joy becomes a witness. Therefore, when we have Christ, we can have joy even though we may not have fame, wealth, power, health, and so on. Ironic that Paul wrote his joyful letter from a prison cell.

Joy in Spite of Circumstances

Third, we can experience joy *in spite of our circumstances*. Continuing Paul's thought from Philippians, "Rejoice in the Lord *always..."* If we know anything about Paul, we know he lived what he preached. Again, he's writing from prison, not from some luxurious Swiss Alps chalet, sipping lattes. From his confinement in Rome, the apostle still managed to have a *witness of joy*. And why was he in prison? For sharing the Gospel. Paul's circumstances could not dilute or destroy his joy. Instead, it became all the more known.

On another occasion, Paul was imprisoned with his buddy Silas when about midnight they erupted in a full-fledged worship service, praying and singing hymns of thankfulness to God. Meanwhile, all the other prisoners and guards listened in.[20] What a joyful spectacle they must have been. All those other miserable prisoners witnessed the joy of two Fifth-Gospel Christians, and they had to scratch their heads and wonder how these guys could be so positive under such dire circumstances.

Finally, Paul repeats his command for emphasis and importance. He writes, "Rejoice in the Lord always; again I will say, rejoice." He knows how forgetful we are. Paul thinks, *In case I wasn't clear enough, let me say it again—rejoice, Christian!* Can you sense his urgency? Can you feel it?

Let's face it. Life often gets the best of us. We get caught up in the same rat race as everyone else and forget what and Who we're living for. But no matter what happens to us, we are not hostages to our emotions or prisoners to our circumstances. We are overcomers.

The Joy Stealers

So what about you? What regularly robs you of your joy? What thieves sneak into your heart-home and make off with your valuable treasure of joy in Jesus? Maybe you can pick out some of the usual suspects in the lineup of joy-stealing criminals.

Thief 1: Busyness

You become so preoccupied with the tasks and to-dos of daily life that your joy is slowly drained out of you.

Thief 2: Relational Tensions

People, including your spouse, coworkers, classmates, room-mates, children, parents, and friends, can suck the emotional life out of you. So your joy has to be rooted in something stronger than human relationships. Something that resupplies you from the inside out.[21]

Thief 3: Financial Stress

Unless you're independently wealthy, you suffer from this tension. And even if you are wealthy, you deal with the constant stress of managing your money, keeping it safe, and continuing to make more. Who doesn't stress over bills, debt, job security, making ends meet? Could the joy of Christ be so awesome that it sustains you through the worst that life can throw at you? Can you live with financial tension and still have amazing joy?

Thief 4: Religious Living Versus Relational Living

The prophet Jeremiah wrote,

> Your words were found, and I ate them,
>   and your words became to me a joy
>   and the delight of my heart,
> for I am called by your name,
>   O Lord, God of hosts.[22]

At its core, religion is man-centered. It's an effort to perform some religious duty or achieve a moral standard. But religious living is joyless, and here's why: we can never consistently attain to those standards, no matter how hard we try. We are never good enough.

On the flip side, a relationship with God brings acceptance and grace, a personal intimacy with Someone we know and trust. That's why Jeremiah could receive and consume God's Word as a hungry man does food. That's why His words were a joy for him. As a new-born baby craving mother's milk, we naturally long for God's truth.[23] We don't dread it or reject it. We scream for it. It's a joy to receive. The happiest time of a baby's day is when the milk arrives.

Why isn't God's Word like that to more Christians? Are we cutting off our nourishing supply of joy by not receiving the Word as Jeremiah did? That's what relationship will do for us. Religion without relationship is empty.

Are we cutting off our nourishing supply of joy by not receiving God's Word?

Thief 5: Sin

Ah yes, the *s*-word. One of the reasons we sin is that we believe the lie that it'll bring us happiness and pleasure. And it actually might for a moment or a season. So, let's concede the point that sin can be fun—temporarily. It *can* bring a temporary sense of happiness. But like Moses, we can make the tough decisions to give up the momentary pleasures of sin in order to experience the everlasting pleasures of God.[24] Even after great sin and forfeiting our joy in God, we can ask Him to "Restore to me the joy of your salvation."[25] And He does.

Every time.

There's a portrait hanging in my office called *Laughing Jesus*. I'm looking at it right now as I write. I love it because it's a picture of my Savior reveling in contagious joy, far different from those emotionally sterile paintings of a contemplative, philosopher-teacher. Jesus oozed joy. And though He was certainly a "man of sorrows and acquainted with grief,"[26] I believe Jesus was the most joyful person who ever lived.

As we saw in an earlier chapter, the Bible says of God the Father speaking about the Son, "You have loved righteousness and hated wickedness; therefore, God, your God, has anointed you with the oil of gladness *beyond your companions.*"[27] How could Jesus be more joyful than His companions? Because He wasn't bogged down with the guilt that comes with sin. He

With Christ as our example, we can experience and display joy no matter what life throws our way.

loved righteousness and hated lawlessness. The Father was His *summum bonum.*

Even under the shadow of the cross, we see a Jesus "who *for the joy that was set before him* endured the cross, despising the shame, and is seated at the right hand of the throne of God."[28] And just how could Jesus be joyful on His way to the cross? He knew that His death would save billions of lost souls—including you and me. He knew His death would ultimately destroy the works of the devil. But He also knew He'd soon be back at the Father's right hand, where He rightfully belongs. With Christ as our example, we can experience and display joy no matter what life throws our way.

William Barclay, the Scottish theologian, said, "We are chosen for joy. However hard the Christian life may be, it is the way of joy. A gloomy Christian is a classic contradiction, and perhaps nothing has done Christianity more harm than overly serious believers with long faces."

We have to change that.

Believer, never lose sight of this: *the degree to which you enjoy God will be the degree to which God is exalted through your life.* The Westminister Shorter Catechism reminds us, "The chief end of man is to glorify God and enjoy Him forever." He is glorified the most by those who enjoy Him the most. Find your delight in God and people will notice. That joy is what God uses to show the world He is desirable and worthy of worship.

If you've lost your joy, ask God to revive your heart. This was the psalmist's cry,

> Will you not revive us again,
>   that your people may rejoice in you?[29]

God will revive you and give you a joy that spills over into every area of your life. That's what Paul was getting at when he wrote, "So, whether you eat or drink, or whatever you do, do all to the glory of God."[30]

This isn't just for Sundays…it's for when we're driving, walking, working out, eating dinner, playing, or whatever we're doing. Joy is the natural result of receiving the Good News and being controlled by God's Spirit.[31]

Solomon said life under the sun is "vanity of vanities." He had it all: wealth, honor, fame, power, health, pleasure, virtue (wisdom), but without God, life is empty. Meaningless. Futile. Solomon knew real joy didn't reside under the sun but beyond it—with God.

If it's true that we become like what we worship, then the more we worship our joy-filled Christ, the more our joy will become evident to all. And that's exactly what a watching world is dying to witness.

GOSPEL APPEALS

- *Negative Christians give bad press to Christianity.*
- *Authentic joy makes our faith desirable.*
- *The degree to which you enjoy God will be the degree to which God is exalted through your life.*

Questions for Further Thought and Discussion

1. Bobby said, "I believe the church should be the most joyful place in the world." Do you believe that?

2. Since we spend so much time and effort seeking joy, do you think we really believe true joy is found only in Jesus? If so, why do we seek it from Him so rarely?

3. Would people describe you as a joyful person? If not, what's stealing your joy?

4. What does it say about God that we are commanded to be joyful (see Philippians 4:4)?

5. Bobby talks about joy being the missing link in evangelism today. It's a secret weapon. Do you agree? Why or why not?

6. What is the greatest object of your joy? Your job, your kids, your spouse, yourself, God, something else?

7. Paul said, "For to me to live is Christ, and to die is gain" (Philippians 1:21). How about you? How would you fill in this verse? "For to me to live is _____, and to die is _____"? What is it "to live" for you?

Chapter 6

THE VOICE OF SUFFERING

"The blood of the martyrs is the seed of the church."

TERTULLIAN, EARLY CHURCH FATHER

On December 4, 1982, Australians Boris and Duska became the proud parents of a baby boy. The baby, whom they named Nick, was like every other Aussie newborn except for one thing—he had no arms and legs. Just stumps. In spite of this, little Nick grew up with a determination to overcome his massive handicap. With only a few toes on his left foot, he taught himself to type…up to forty-five words per minute. He soon learned to throw a tennis ball, play drum pedals, brush his teeth, comb his hair, and even surf, swim, and snorkel. Oh, and he tackled skydiving too.

As if that's not impressive enough, Nick went on to earn a college degree. He eventually married, and today he and his wife, Kanae, have a son. One visit to his website and you are immediately struck by his refreshingly optimistic attitude. Nick's blog is called *Attitude Is Altitude,* where every visitor is greeted with:

> Hi Friend,
>
> My name is Nick Vujicic and I am thankful to have

been born 30 years ago with no arms and no legs. I won't pretend my life is easy, but through the love of my parents, loved ones, and faith in God, I have overcome my adversity and my life is now filled with joy and purpose.[1]

Today, Nick Vujicic travels the world as a motivational speaker, encouraging people not to give up in difficult circumstances. But beyond that, he points people to the Lord Jesus Christ through his amazing life and experience of suffering. Nick shamelessly took the opportunity in front of an Oprah Winfrey live audience to unapologetically make much of his Savior, Jesus Christ.[2] His inspiring YouTube videos have been watched over one hundred million times.

Nick's amazing story teaches us as Christians that no matter how hard life gets, we have a message to share. His example makes me think about the petty little things that hinder and burden my life from time to time. I stand corrected and inspired by Nick's powerful God-centered and Christ-sharing example. The title of his book, *Life Without Limits: Inspiration for a Ridiculously Good Life*, oozes Nick's resiliant approach to life. Nick Vujicic is a man who has learned to suffer well.

But imagine for a moment if Nick's ultrasound could have been viewed by the world. Would a large percentage have encouraged his parents to abort him? Most people with far fewer physical disabilities than Nick's would have given up a long time ago. But not this Aussie. In truth, Nick's already outlived most of us by a long shot—even without limbs.

> God can be glorified *through our suffering.*

What Nick Vujicic came to realize is that God can be glorified *through his suffering.* That his limitations had a higher purpose. Many people use suffering as an argument against God's existence or against Him being good. But Nick's voice carries powerful credibility when it comes to suffering.

If God Is Good...

To be fair, though, I do hear the skeptic's argument here. It goes something like this:

A. If God is all-powerful, He can get rid of suffering.

B. If God is all-good and all-loving, He will get rid of suffering. But guess what?

C. Suffering still exists; therefore God must be neither all-powerful, nor all-loving.

There are several reasons why this argument is flawed. The argument's foundation is cracked and built on faulty and incomplete logic. Let's examine it more carefully.

Point A—we wholeheartedly agree with this. God is all-powerful and able to end suffering. No problem. So far so good.

Point B—we also agree with this...in God's time. While God will eventually do away with suffering, the framer of the argument commits a huge error here. First, he pretends to know the timing of God's end to suffering. Considering the limited nature of human understanding, this is, at best, presumptuous and at worst, arrogant. The second error he makes is to assume that mankind somehow *deserves* to be relieved of all suffering, as if God *owes* us health, happiness, and a pain-free life here on earth. But as we read Scripture, we actually discover the opposite to be true.[3]

The third logical error is a failure to allow for the possibility that an all-powerful, all-wise, all-loving, and good God who possesses an infinite mind *may* have a higher purpose for present suffering that:

• He's not currently sharing with us

• cannot presently be known and understood

• can be known and understood only by some

• can only be partially understood by some or all

• will be revealed at a future time

Thinking he has trapped the Christian into an intellectual/theological corner, in reality the skeptic has effectively done the equivalent of showing a very weak hand in a game of poker.

So with a higher line of reasoning coupled with Scripture, we're going to affirm that God does indeed have a purpose for suffering and one that, at least in part, can be known when He chooses to reveal it.

> We don't have a lot of patience for suffering...we seek to eliminate it every chance we get.

But let's first agree together on another common truth. Suffering is no fun. It's no walk in the park. We do whatever it takes to avoid it, right? In America we don't have a lot of patience for suffering. Suffering is devalued, so we seek to eliminate it every chance we get. We pride ourselves on having good health, making money, climbing the corporate ladder, and being successful. But have you considered that some suffering is a theological necessity in a fallen world? What if it's an inherent part of our existence? What if pain, sickness, loss, and death were somehow a tool in God's hands? Perhaps a sacred thorn? Not wasted but part of the required course load on our way toward Christlikeness?

What if suffering actually has an aim? A purpose. A point. Thankfully, this is true for those who know Christ. We do not suffer randomly or without purpose. There is nothing random or purposeless with a Sovereign God and His ways. Otherwise, God appears like some sadomasochist who derives pleasure through inflicting pain on His creatures. There is something inherent within us that longs to understand why we suffer, especially suffering that is not a direct consequence of sin. As we try to make sense of it all, Satan capitalizes on our questions and confusion and attempts to drive a wedge of doubt between God and us. And what makes it doubly difficult is that God seldom answers all our whys.

So What's the Point?

The Greeks had a word—*apologia*—from which we get our word *apologetics*, meaning to "give a defense." The study of apologetics is the ability to give a rational, credible defense for our faith. But it's more than merely stuffing our heads with finely tuned arguments. Rather, it involves a multitude of convincing life witnesses. One of those witnesses is how we manage suffering. For the believer, suffering is never silent. It always has a voice. The question is, "Which voice?"

Our lives never have more potential influence for Christ than when we suffer well. Suffering naturally leads us downward toward self-pity, depression, and even bitterness. But processing our pain ought to go way beyond that, and deeper insight is available to those who know God and His Word.

> Our lives never have more potential influence for Christ than when we suffer well.

I believe it's critically important to know how to intellectually defend our faith. I'm all for it, 100 percent. In my widely used online ministry, "The One-Minute Apologist," I give succinct answers to important questions in a creative format.[4] I've had the privilege of interviewing some of the greatest Christian apologists in the world today. Some of the questions we tackle are:

- "If God is good, why is there evil?"
- "Is the Bible trustworthy?"
- "What about those who have never heard about Jesus Christ? Will they be saved?"
- "Are miracles possible?"

We address hundreds of tough questions people ask, so you can confidently defend your faith *intellectually*. But people are far more convinced by our *life* than by our *brains*. If others see that we are the real deal, then they might conclude that our beliefs are also just as genuine. We cannot divorce our heads from our hearts, our lips from our life, and our intelligence from our influence. Instead, we need a combination of these realities coming together, testifying to the credibility of the Christian faith.

Making an Impact Through Suffering

With that in mind, would it surprise you if I told you the main verse dealing with Christian apologetics has to do with making a life impact—through *suffering*?[5] The apostle Peter encourages us, "But in your hearts honor Christ the Lord as holy, always being prepared to make a defense (*apologia*) to anyone who asks you for a reason for the hope that is in you; yet do it with gentleness and respect."

This verse is loaded with meaning and life-changing application. Peter urges these early Christians (and us) to be ready to speak up when given the opportunity to share our faith. He basically says, "Hey guys, when others ask you to share why you are so hopeful, don't hesitate to tell them the reason why you have this hope within you." But what makes this verse extra powerful is the context in which it is found. To effectively interpret Scripture, we must understand it in its original context. Context is the key that opens the door to understanding God's Word. And this verse is set in a context of Christian suffering, specifically suffering through persecution.

> As long as suffering is for righteousness' sake, we have a golden opportunity to shine for Christ in the midst of it.

Peter is writing to a group of exiles, coaching them on how to suffer well through *hope*. He reasons that as long as suffering is for righteousness' sake, we have a golden opportunity to shine for Christ in the midst of it.

Obviously, not all suffering happens this way. Some suffering is self-induced by poor choices, sin, and rejecting God's ways. That's not the kind of suffering Peter is talking about. Previously, he had written, "But even if you should suffer for righteousness' sake, you will be blessed. Have no fear of them, nor be troubled."[6] That's a verse that's a lot easier to *write* than to *live*. But it's not beyond our ability in Christ to do so.

Peter is telling these first-century Christians not to fear, but to keep their hope in
Jesus Christ. And why? So they can be a witness for Jesus in their suffering. Suffering

Suffering opens
the door for us to
brag on Jesus.

with hope gives us an opportunity to distinguish our lives from the lives of nonbelievers in a positive way. It opens the door for us to brag on Jesus. Peter is saying, "There is a way you can live that causes your life to invite questions." You could say that when we suffer well, our lives speak for themselves.

And how?

It communicates strength in the midst of weakness.

It stirs curiosity. ("How can you be so positive in light of your circumstances?")

It creates wonder in a watching world.

Additionally, when we share our faith while suffering, Peter urges us to do so with "gentleness and respect."[7] William Lane Craig, the great Christian apologist and philosopher, reminds us, "We can present a *defense* of the Christian faith without becoming *defensive*. We can present *arguments* for Christianity without becoming *argumentative*."[8]

The late Dr. Howard Hendricks was one of my favorite profes-
sors at Dallas Theological Seminary, a position he held for over sixty years. He once told the story about a flight attendant who was living a Fifth-Gospel life. Dr. Hendricks was sitting in a plane that was delayed for take off, and as the wait dragged on, the passen-
gers became more and more annoyed. Hendricks noticed how gra-
cious one of the flight attendants was as she spoke with her agitated travelers. Her tone was gentle and respectful despite the passen-
gers' growing irritability. After the plane was finally airborne, Hen-
dricks told the flight attendant how amazed he was at her poise and self-control, and he said he wanted to write a letter of commenda-
tion for her to the airline. The stewardess smiled, replying that she

didn't work for the airline company but for Jesus Christ. She told Dr. Hendricks that before going to work, she and her husband had prayed together, asking God to help her be a good representative of Christ.

Attitude matters.

And so do our reactions to life's circumstances.

Suffering through irritations, unpleasant experiences, pains, and even persecutions can be a powerful and convincing tool in the hands of God. It's a clarion voice of testimony, broadcasting to our family, friends, and world that Jesus and His sustaining love are real and available…and that it *works*.

So what have we said so far?

- Our voice in suffering is heard when we keep an optimistic outlook (Nick Vujicic).

- Our voice in suffering is heard when our hope is in Jesus (1 Peter 3:15).

- Our voice in suffering is heard when we react well (Prof Hendricks's story).

One of the challenges for today's Christians is that we are either ignorant of or fail to connect with our great Christian heritage. This is partially due to the time and centuries that separate us, and it's unfortunate because there's so much inspiration to gain from those who have stood for Christ throughout history. One of those inspirations is a man named William Tyndale.

> There is much inspiration to gain from those who have stood for Christ throughout history.

A sixteenth-century English scholar, Tyndale was arrested, imprisoned, and convicted for translating the Bible into the English language. He was subsequently sentenced to death, his life coming to a brutal end as he was strangled while tied to a stake. Following his martyrdom, his executioners burned his body. But William Tyndale died giving glory to God. With his last words, he cried out,

"Lord, open the king of England's eyes." John Foxe in his famous *Foxe's Book of Martyrs* said of this Fifth-Gospel man, "Such was the power of his doctrine, and the sincerity of his life, that during the time of his imprisonment (which endured a year and a half), he converted, it is said, his keeper, the keeper's daughter, and others of his household."[9]

There probably isn't much of a chance you'll be burned at the stake for your faith, but God still gives you opportunities to shine His light through your particular suffering. It's not really a matter of if, but when.

> God gives you opportunities to shine His light through your particular suffering.

Suffering, My Friend?

What if you could take a pill and in a matter of minutes have all the patience you need? What if there were a drink that would fill you with compassion, wisdom, and perseverance? Would you drink it? Would you purchase it for $9.99? How fast would you order it online?

Okay, now imagine that God offers you all those things, only they don't come through a pill or a drink. Rather, they come through periodic *suffering*. How eager are you to swipe your credit card for that one? Doesn't that sound like an exciting, one-of-a-kind offer? Not sold in stores! How well do you think an offer like this would sell?

But that's exactly what James (a half-brother of Jesus) explains to us in his epistle: "Consider it pure joy, my brothers and sisters, whenever you face trials of many kinds, because you know that the testing of your faith produces perseverance. Let perseverance finish its work so that you may be mature and complete, not lacking anything."[10]

But how could *anyone* think about life's problems and suffering as "pure joy"? That sounds a bit paradoxical, don't you think? It seems a bit sadomasochistic to "welcome suffering." There's something very unnatural about that. Maybe a little twisted. So...why would anyone do this?

Suffering and the Building of Character

One of the things we discover as we follow Jesus is not only are His ways not our ways, but that they almost always seem opposite from conventional thinking. In Christianity, leaders are those who serve others; real love is when you bless those who curse you; we love, not hate, our enemies. Following Jesus means that the only way to live is to die. To be exalted you must humble yourself.

This "backward" teaching of Jesus goes on and on. And it continues when it comes to suffering. While nowhere in the Bible does it ever tell us to *seek* suffering, when unavoidable suffering does come knocking on our door, we answer it, asking God for wisdom to navigate through it for as long as it lasts.

> As weight training develops muscle, so trials build up important areas of our character.

Suffering is like a sudden storm. Unexpected. Unwanted. Inconvenient. Annoying. Disruptive. And yet, there is something *in* the storm for us. Not just a "life lesson," but something more substantial than that. We don't get spiritual truths primarily from the testing of our faith; rather, from the testing of our faith we get the development of our spirit. Our entire personhood is affected. As weight training develops muscle, so trials are sent or allowed in order to build up important areas of our character. And apparently God cares deeply about developing who we are.

As we process our suffering, we make specific choices to exercise those spiritual muscles. Like any workout, this often is a painful process. Not fun. And you can experience soreness afterward. But if you stay with it, seeking God's wisdom through the storm, you will emerge on the other side with something you didn't have before. Things like wisdom, perseverance, and maturity—the things every Christ-follower passionately desires.

> You can't microwave yourself into maturity.

There are no quick-and-easy ways to these results. No shortcuts. No fast track to the top. No express lanes. No drive-through discipleship. You can't microwave yourself into maturity. Instead, it happens in our pain. Over time.

But here's the cool part. Jesus walks with you and stays by your side throughout your storm. Like the disciples' experience on the Sea of Galilee, Jesus remains in your boat.[11] You're not going to sink as long as you keep your eyes on Him. Sometimes Jesus calms the storm and other times He just calms you! But if you have the Son of God with you in your darkest hours, you're safe.[12] The key is to surrender to God's calming touch. And again, what we get on the back end far outweighs what we go through.[13]

In addition to what James tells us, suffering can do even more things for us. For example, suffering gives us *perspective*. Suffering can bury our spirits or clarify our thinking. It boils down to a choice we get to make. When we suffer with Christ by our side, we see things from a different vantage point. Suffering has a unique way of detoxing our perspective, clearing up our vision, and wiping our mental windshield. We relearn what's really important in life.

How many times have you heard someone recount that after a life trauma—a serious illness, losing a home in a fire, surviving a car accident—that they have a renewed appreciation for life, breath, and those close to them. They got perspective on the things that really matter.

Suffering also can deliver us from complacency, mediocrity, and spiritual flat-lining. Ironically, suffering can prevent us from experiencing a slow spiritual death, even though it may itself seem like a slow death. Instead, it often serves as a wake-up call, a spiritual alarm clock that jolts us out of slumber and back into reality and the path to growth. Beyond this, it cleanses our senses, enabling us to draw upon God's power and resources like never before.

As you survey Scripture, you find a lot of people who called out to God in their hour of suffering and need (David, Moses, Elijah, Daniel, Peter, Paul, to name a few). Even Jesus, in His hour of betrayal and death, called out to the Father for help. It was in this moment that an angel was sent to minister to Him, strengthening the God-Man for the journey, mission, and suffering He had been called to.[14]

Which introduces us to another benefit we gain through suffering. Look at what the author of Hebrews says about this:

> In the days of his flesh, Jesus offered up prayers and sup-plications, with loud cries and tears, to him who was able to save him from death, and he was heard because of his reverence. Although he was a son, he learned obedience through what he suffered. And being made per-fect, he became the source of eternal salvation to all who obey him, being designated by God a high priest after the order of Melchizedek.[15]

It may be a bit confusing to think about Jesus, who is God incar-nate, "*learning* obedience." Wasn't He already perfect and obedient to the Father? Well yes, but in order to qualify as our Savior, Jesus chose to trust in the Father, and in His humanity "learn" certain things. Though He was the eternal Son of God, as a Man He still had to grow, develop, and discover.[16] And part of that discovery was learning to obey through suffering.

Suffering can teach us to obey God by faith.

Face it; anyone can obey when things are going well. A smooth path is easy to walk on. But add some rocks, valleys, potholes, and thorns and obedience becomes a much more difficult choice. Jesus is our perfect example for this as the Author and Perfecter of our faith.[17] So suffering can teach us to obey God *by faith*, sometimes without much understanding. And this is exactly the kind of faith that pleases God.[18]

Suffering and God's Sovereignty

Further, as Christians we believe our God is sovereign. This means He is in control of the universe, and that nothing escapes His notice. It also means that, in the grand scheme of things, nothing really happens by accident. God's power and rule superintend all things. And though we may not be privy to His counsel,[19] we can be confident in His promise to "work all things together for good to those who love God.[20]

This means that every difficult circumstance and all the suffering we face has to get permission from God before coming into our lives. If we place our faith in His Word and character, suffering will become a part of our story, a story of becoming like our Master. Tightly woven into the fabric of our lives, our sufferings become like bulletproof Kevlar, protecting us from the things that would harm us. This trust in God's sovereignty produces a calm assurance that, even in the raging storm, all is well.

> Trust in God's sovereignty produces a calm assurance that, even in the raging storm, all is well.

Again, this kind of thinking isn't some sort of morbid death wish or obsession with pain. It's simply saying that when we encounter trials and suffering, we can be sure they can be used toward our progress in God. As powerful as the suffering is, equally powerful are the ways we can grow as we endure it.

But I am compelled to add a final thought about enduring suffering, We are often tempted to view suffering as punishment from God, as if we've done something to make Him mad. But God's punishment for us was exhausted at the cross. As a result, "there is now *no condemnation* for those who are in Christ Jesus."[21] You have been declared holy in God's sight, spotless before His throne.[22] Our entire Christian life is spent understanding, practicing, and experiencing what that means.

One of the ways God does this is through disciplining us. Again, not as punishment but more like a good coach, placing us in situations and circumstances that test and train us toward success and His ultimate plan for our lives. And our loving Father is committed both to us and to this glorious process.[23] Once again, the brilliant author of Hebrews writes,

> It is for discipline that you have to endure. God is treating you as sons. For what son is there whom his father

does not discipline? If you are left without discipline, in which all have participated, then you are illegitimate children and not sons. Besides this, we have had earthly fathers who disciplined us and we respected them. Shall we not much more be subject to the Father of spirits and live? For they disciplined us for a short time as it seemed best to them, but he disciplines us for our good, that we may share his holiness. For the moment all discipline seems painful rather than pleasant, but later it yields the peaceful fruit of righteousness to those who have been trained by it.[24]

A "fruit of righteousness"? Can you imagine this? That through your response to suffering and discipline, God would transform your mind and heart so that His righteous character is clearly seen in us by others. And even here our most excellent Jesus is the perfect model for living this way. He gives us hope and keeps us from losing heart.[25]

So think about it. Through suffering, you get to become a walking advertisement for the greatness and power of God. And if that wasn't enough, you gain wisdom, perseverance, maturity, God's close presence, perspective, spiritual alertness, obedience, a calm assurance, and a harvest of righteousness.

What child of God wouldn't want all that?

God never looks more beautiful through our lives than when we suffer well, when even in the silence of pain, a voice within us still speaks up. Have you ever considered the thought that perhaps the suffering you're currently resisting could be the very tool God uses to help you share Jesus with others? It could be the very tool that grabs the attention of the nonbelieving onlooker situated at a place near you.

Suffer well, my friend. Let everyone know of the strong hope within you. A hope they desperately need.

GOSPEL APPEALS

- *Suffering is as much an opportunity as it is an obstacle.*
- *If you're looking for a role model on how to suffer, look no further than Jesus.*

Questions for Further Thought and Discussion

1. Share a time when you saw a Christian suffer well. What kind of impact did that person have on you?

2. Do you think when Christians suffer well, it's really an opportunity for them to be distinguished in the world?

3. Doesn't suffering seem like a rather high price to pay to be a witness? Why or why not?

4. What are some other benefits that can come into our life as a result of suffering?

5. Have you ever suffered for the sake of the Gospel or known anyone who has? Explain.

6. If you are discussing this book in a small group, allow some time for those in the group to describe any struggles or suffering they are going through. Then spend some time praying for each other.

Chapter 7

FOOLS FOR CHRIST

"We are fools for Christ's sake."

Paul the apostle

U nless you happen to be from another planet, you probably own or know someone who owns an Apple product. Even so, it's likely you've never heard the name Ken Segall. Ken was the creative wizard and director behind Apple's widely successful and innovative "Think Different" campaign, which won just about every award imaginable.

The "Crazy Ones"

In sixty-second TV spots, Apple featured such notable figures as Albert Einstein, Bob Dylan, Amelia Earhart, Martin Luther King Jr., John Lennon, Alfred Hitchcock, Mahatma Gandhi, Jim Henson, Pablo Picasso, and Thomas Edison. Viewers heard the voice of veteran actor Richard Dreyfuss say,

> Here's to the crazy ones. The misfits. The rebels. The troublemakers. The round pegs in the square holes. The ones who see things differently. They're not fond of rules, and they have no respect for the status quo. You

can quote them, disagree with them, glorify or vilify them. About the only thing you can't do is ignore them. Because they change things. They push the human race forward. And while some see them as the crazy ones, we see genius. Because the people who are crazy enough to think they can change the world...are the ones who do.

The ad concluded with the words "Think Different" against a black background. Then the Apple logo slowly appeared.

Pure genius. Brilliant.

And Apple quickly went from brilliant to *billions*. The "Think Different" campaign was meant to inspire. But beyond that, it was meant to draw you in, to create an association between the great adventurers/thinkers/philosophers/artists/inventors...and Apple. And to make you want to join in on the genius. Perhaps you're one of the more than eighty-five million who have bought an iPhone or some other Apple product.[1]

Ah, the sweet smell of success.

> The Bible is filled with men and women who challenged the status quo.

As I read my Bible, I find it filled with men and women who, like those highlighted in Apple's ad campaign, challenged the status quo. They took the conventional thinking of the day and tossed it out the window like yesterday's garbage. In its place, they took the road less traveled. Most of the time they took the road *never* traveled.

Weird Ways

It appears that God actually delights in distinguishing His followers from the rest of humanity, frequently doing so in unusual, seemingly ridiculous ways. As we examine Scripture carefully, we discover an undercurrent that runs throughout. God asks His children to do things that are, to be honest, nonsensical, foolish, silly, offensive, and absurd. He asks us to embrace the ridiculous. For example:

- *God promised Abraham he'd be the father of many nations. Then, after Abraham finally receives his promised son, God tells him to kill the child.*

Any way you look at it, this plan doesn't makes sense. From our perspective it's downright offensive and even immoral. But hidden from Abraham's understanding was that this was only a test. A very serious one. God knows that most anyone obeys Him when blessing is promised and given. But what about when that long-awaited gift is delivered and God asks you to give it back? How many obey then? In this case, it must have seemed to Abraham, at least at first, that God was betraying not only him but also His own Word. Strange indeed, and yet God knew what He was doing.

- *In order to conquer Jericho, God told Joshua to have Israel's army march around the walls of that city once each day for six days, and then, on the seventh day, to march around it seven times.*[2]

On the final day, the priests would blow trumpets and the walls would come crashing down. Does that sound like an effective battle strategy to you? Imagine a conversation between two Israeli foot soldiers that day.

> *Soldier 1*: "So let me get this straight—he wants us to hike in circles around the city every day for seven days?"
>
> *Soldier 2*: "Right. Then after that, the army brass section is gonna blow their horns, and the walls will fall down flat."
>
> *Soldier 1*: I don't know, Eli. I've been looking in the field manual, and I can't find the section on trumpets being used as weapons. Am I missing something here?"
>
> *Soldier 2*: "Simeon, ours is not to question why, only to do or die."
>
> *Soldier 1*: "You got that right."

General Joshua and his army must have looked ridiculous before the watching eyes of the inhabitants of Jericho. Surely they mocked them from atop the city walls. Meanwhile, Joshua's own men must have secretly wondered if they were marching to their death. Nevertheless, Joshua obeyed the seemingly foolish command. And the walls fell.

- *God commanded Ezekiel to publicly lie down on his left side for 390 days, then flip over and lie on his right side for another 40 days.*

Was this some new diet fad? Ancient yoga? I mean, it's one thing to do something crazy like that within the privacy of your home, but publicly? Why this bizarre behavior? God was using Ezekiel to teach onlookers a lesson. It had something to do with symbolically bearing Israel's sin. Ezekiel was to be a living illustration, a sideways sidewalk sign, like staging a public protest today. We often refer to people like this as being "off their rocker." If I were a betting man, I would wager that a lot of people laughed at Ezekiel.

- *Isaiah was commanded to walk naked for three years to get his message across.*

"At that time the LORD spoke by Isaiah the son of Amoz, saying, 'Go, and loose the sackcloth from your waist and take off your sandals from your feet,' and he did so, walking naked and barefoot."[3] If someone came into my church office and said, "Pastor Bobby, God spoke to me last night and said I'm supposed to walk through Charlotte buck naked so as to picture Charlotte's nakedness before God," I'd think, *This dude's nuts,* and immediately recommend professional counseling. I thought this stuff happened only at Cal State Berkeley, not in the Bible.

Can you imagine Isaiah's thoughts after hearing this call? "Um, God are You sure about this? You said 'naked,' right?" And this went on for *three years.*[4] Isaiah served as an object lesson of how both the

Egyptians and the Cushites would be treated by the powerful Assyrians. All that just to make a point? Hello? Sunscreen anyone?[5]

- *Naaman, the leper was instructed to dip in the Jordan
  River seven times to be cured.*[6]

This solution seemed extremely foolish to Naaman, so much so that he left Elisha's house in a rage. The Bible says,

> Naaman was angry and went away, saying, "Behold, I thought that he would surely come out to me and stand and call upon the name of the LORD his God, and wave his hand over the place and cure the leper. Are not Abana and Pharpar, the rivers of Damascus, better than all the waters of Israel? Could I not wash in them and be clean?" So he turned and went away in a rage.[7]

Namaan, the nonbelieving army commander, was being taught a little lesson about how God "thinks different." But if he wanted to see God work, he would have to humble himself and trust God's ways. Naaman's servants helped him to chill out, and soon he acquiesced, setting his dignity aside and doing what seemed foolish. The result? Complete healing.

- *Gideon's army was reduced from over thirty thousand
  down to three hundred.*[8]

God shrank Gideon's army down to three hundred before they went to battle against the Midianites. Now there's a church growth strategy for you! God wanted Gideon to know that in order for his faith to be placed in the right object, he had to drastically reduce the size of his army so he wouldn't give any of the credit to himself or to the strength of his military force. Conventional warfare in Gideon's day (as in ours) was "might makes right," and size *definitely* mattered. At the end of the day, the army that walked off the battlefield alive was typically the larger one.

So this military tactic seemed to Gideon like nothing more than a recipe for mass slaughter. He would be remembered as the dumbest, most backward-thinking commander in Israel's history. Or would he? The Bible records, "The LORD said to Gideon, 'The people with you are too many for me to give the Midianites into their hand, lest Israel boast over me, saying, "My own hand has saved me."'"[9] To any watching eye, then or now, this three-hundred-man army had to look absurd. But 300 + God = victory. And Gideon and his men won the battle.

- *Jesus sent His disciples out on a mission with next to nothing.*

Lest you think this kind of thinking was just an Old Testament thing, it continued into the first century. Jesus charged His disciples to "take nothing for their journey except a staff—no bread, no bag, no money in their belts—but to wear sandals and not put on two tunics."[10] But God, what about raising financial support first? Maybe a carry-on? Perhaps some trail mix? Nothing?

- *Jesus told His disciples where they should throw their nets, even though they had been fishing all night without catching anything.*[11]

Now it may have been okay for Jesus to recommend some quirky ideas when it came to spiritual things and ministry, but now He's claiming to be an expert on fishing too? And it's not like He can fake this one. He's talking to *professional fishermen*. Was Jesus out of His league here? Apparently not. They caught so many fish they couldn't even haul in the net.

- *Jesus asked His disciples to bring Him some bread and a few fish to feed a multitude.*[12]

This had to have been one of the most absurd, even embarrassing, requests Jesus ever made of His followers. Scripture tells us about five thousand *men* were there that day. When you add the estimated number of women and children who were also on the mountainside, you arrive at a number closer to fifteen to twenty thousand. And all the disciples could produce were five loaves of bread and two scrawny fish. That's hardly enough for one hungry teenager.

But little is much when God is in it, especially when the Lord Himself exercises His wonder-working power. Jesus didn't want to give that massive crowd just a snack. He wanted to give them something to remember, so He gave them a feast. And they all ate "as much as they wanted." Their bellies were filled, or as we say in the South, they were "full as a tick." (I know. Gross.)

- *The apostle Paul was blinded by a vision of Jesus, and then told to go to the home of Ananias, a complete stranger, who would lay his hands on him to be healed.*[13]

Now that may not sound too odd to you, unless you consider that just twenty-four hours earlier, Paul would have either arrested or killed Ananias on the spot. And Ananias knew this. That's why God had to give him a special vision to convince him to accept Paul as a brother. Imagine God telling you to open your front door and embrace a radical jihadist. How willing would you be? Would you be skeptical? Confused? Fearful? Maybe want to seek a second opinion?

> God has quite the reputation for asking His children to do things that are out of the ordinary.

So it would seem God has quite the reputation for asking His children to do things that are, to put it mildly, out of the ordinary. Things that to everyone else appear unwise and even downright stupid. This falls into the category of "For my thoughts are not your thoughts, neither are your ways my ways, declares the LORD."[14] That's "thinking different." God goes on to say through Isaiah that there is an infinite gap between the way *He* thinks and the way *we* think.

Think about that.

But God's creative, out-of-the-box ideas not only challenge our thinking but also test our faith. We Christians are quick to sing and talk about trusting God and following Him no matter what. But when He asks something odd, difficult, or uncomfortable of us, that's when things get a bit complicated.

I have heard it said, "It's okay to be a nut as long as you are screwed on the right bolt." So, here's a question for you: When was the last time someone told you that being nuts was a mark of a Christ-follower? Feels borderline insane, right? I mean, who wants to be called a nutcase? Doesn't the world have enough wack jobs? But before you close this book and go back to browsing Facebook, hang with me. If it makes you feel better, we can tone down the word. Instead of being *nuts*, how about being a *fool* for Christ? That's the word Paul uses. Does that sound better? Probably not.

Never before has the church tried so hard to fit in with society.

But here's where we find ourselves today. Never before has the church tried so hard to fit in with society, when in reality God still wants us to think different and stand out. We've spent so much time, energy, and money trying to convince the world that we're *normal*—just like them. And why? Because deep down we want to be accepted by our friends and culture. And this stems from two roots—an insecurity about our faith and a subtle fear of man. Both of these contribute to our desperation to be liked. And neither are characteristic of the Fifth-Gospel Christian.

But here's the problem with this blending-in attitude. Many nonbelievers have concluded, "If you guys are just like me, then why in the world do I need what you have?" Admittedly, we *do* share a great deal in common with unbelievers—we're created and loved by God, we've all sinned, and we each have our own bag of strengths and weaknesses. Many of their life struggles and problems are also our experiences. So we do have common ground that helps us relate to one another.

However, one of the main reasons God saved you and set you apart is so that you wouldn't be *just like* everyone else. There are inherent discernible distinctions between us. God-designed differences. For starters, we're new creations in Christ. The Bible says, "Therefore, if anyone is in Christ, he is a new creation. The old has passed away; behold, the new has come."[15] As Christians, we *are* different. Our identity, our position and standing before God, and our nature all stand in stark contrast to that of the world. Our old way of living has died and a new way of living has been birthed. We think about life in a completely different way. We are now distinguished *and* distinguishable. As a result, a huge part of growing in Christ is the lifelong adventure of matching our behavior to our true nature, identity, and beliefs.

Jesus also likened us to the salt of the earth and the light of the world.[16] That means there is something new and unique about us. Something fresh. Something engaging. Something interesting. We are to be different not just to be different but because we *are* different. And sometimes, we are even called to be *fools*. Of course, we don't intentionally seek to be weird or offensive. We've all seen people like that who give Christ and His followers a bad name. Even so, we still recognize that radical obedience to God may sometimes lead others to think we've gone off the deep end.

> We are to be different not just to be different but because we *are* different.

Why Be Normal?

So how does God practically do this in us? Several ways, actually. The Lord distinguishes us in the world through our character, through our joy, through the way we handle suffering, through our love and weaknesses (as we will soon see), and even through our seemingly foolish lifestyle.

Our devotion to Jesus can often appear unnecessary, misguided, or even ridiculous to an unsaved world. Consider the following from an unbeliever's point of view:

- Why would you get up early on your day off to attend church or a Bible study?

- Why would you sacrifice a well-deserved vacation to feed orphans in Haiti?

- Why would you risk your health to work at a medical clinic in India?

- Why would you spend the energy and money to home-school your kids or pay for a private education when public schools are free?

- Why would you report extra income on your tax return when you can get away with not reporting it?

- Why would you voluntarily give a tenth of your pay-check to God's church when you could spend that on yourself or take a nice vacation?

- Why would you choose to believe an unpopular position on same-sex marriage or abortion? Don't you realize that makes you bigoted and Victorian?

- Why would you tell the truth about discrepancies in your business finances when it could get us all in trouble?

- Why would you leave a well-paying job to go to seminary or into ministry? That seems counterproductive.

- Why would you choose to keep an unwanted child when you can be in and out of a clinic in a couple of hours and go on your merry way? Why would you allow one little mistake to ruin the rest of your life? Are you an idiot?

It doesn't take much to realize the implications of being a

Christ-follower in a post-Christian culture. Sometimes just doing the honest or right thing is viewed as unproductive or primitive.

Prepare for Takeoff

But it's not just our behavior that may appear foolish or offensive to others. It's our *message* as well. In his first letter to the church at Corinth, Paul writes, "For the message of the cross is *foolishness* to those who are perishing."[17] Because people are spiritually blind, they do not possess the ability to receive or believe the message of Jesus and His death on the cross.[18]

It's amazing to consider this, right? But keep in mind, understanding and receiving the Gospel is not a matter of *intelligence*. Rather, it's a matter of *spirituality*. They're not dumb. They're just dead—spiritually.[19] And what can a corpse do except rot?

Many times I've been perplexed why, after I've clearly explained the simple message of God's grace and offer of salvation through Jesus, people still give me that "deer in the headlights" stare. Then I realize that God's Spirit has yet to open their eyes to see their sin and His provision for it.[20] But I pray at least I've planted a seed of truth that God may later use.

Ironically, a few verses later in that same passage Paul adds, "God was pleased through the foolishness of what was preached to save those who believe."[21] So while some think the Gospel message is foolish, others are convinced it actually makes sense, and they believe. As Christians, our lifestyle choices, values, and message often do not make sense to the unbeliever. So this shouldn't come as a surprise to us.

Why does God ask us to do things that seem foolish? Is this some sort of game He's playing with us?

But exactly *why* does God ask us to do things that seem foolish? Is this some sort of game He's playing with us? A test perhaps? Or could there be a more spiritually rational explanation?

Well-known women's speaker and writer Beth Moore tells about an experience she had at an airport while waiting to catch her flight. The terminal was packed to overflowing that day, when suddenly all eyes focused on an elderly man in a wheelchair, pushed along by an airline hostess. This old man had long fingernails and his pants were bunched up, as if he'd lost a lot of weight. His hair was long and stringy and looked as if it hadn't been washed in a long time.

Overwhelmed at the sight of this man, Beth sensed God was up to something. Then a thought popped into her head: *God wants me to witness to this person.* That may have been intimidating enough, but then her heart was immediately filled with fear as she sensed God saying, *Beth, I'm not asking you to witness to him. I'm asking you to go brush his hair.*

All of a sudden witnessing sounded a whole lot easier. *Brush his hair, Lord? Really?* And that's when the internal struggle of excuse-making began. *But I don't even have a hairbrush, God,* she protested.

But the thought refused to leave her mind. And so, as discreetly as possible, Beth walked over and quietly said to the man, "Sir, may I have the honor of brushing your hair?" The old man said, "What?" So she repeated herself a little louder, "May I have the honor of brushing your hair?" The man said, "Lady, if you want me to hear you, then you are going to have to speak up." She must have thought, *God, You're not going to make this easy, are You?* At last, she repeated this ridiculously foolish statement so loud that virtually everyone in the terminal could hear.

"SIR, MAY I HAVE THE PRIVILEGE OF BRUSHING YOUR HAIR?"

Everyone turned and stared. Beth felt humiliated. The old man looked at her and simply said, "If you want to." She thought to herself, *Of course I don't want to,* but instead she replied, "Yes sir, I would love to. But the problem is I don't have a hairbrush." To her surprise, the man said, "I have a hairbrush. It's back in my bag." Stepping around to the back of his wheelchair, Beth bent down and unzipped the little duffle bag. She rummaged through undershirts, pajamas, almost everything in his luggage until finally locating the elusive hairbrush.

By this point, she had become overwhelmed with the love of Christ for this man. Her feelings had shifted from resistance to genuine gratitude to be serving him. And she proceeded to patiently brush the man's matted hair. Beth was so into her mission that she became oblivious to everyone watching, continuing her task until the man's hair was as smooth as silk.

> Beth had become overwhelmed with the love of Christ for this man.

When she had finished, she said to him, "Sir, do you know Jesus?" He replied, "Why yes, I do." Then he confessed with tears in his eyes, "I was just sitting here thinking, 'What a mess I must be for my bride.'" He explained he'd been in a hospital for months and was finally going back home.

The airline hostess soon returned and wheeled the old man onto the airplane. A few minutes later, she came back out with tears streaming down her cheeks. "What made you do that?" she asked. Beth paused and then simply said, "Jesus." And she shared Christ with the lady.

But Beth shared more than words that day in the airport. She proved herself to be a living witness before all who observed her act of kindness. She was a living, observable Gospel for all eyes to see. A Fifth-Gospel Christian—*in action*. What had initially felt so ridiculous turned out to be a very beautiful thing. What began as foolishness was in reality an appropriate gesture of love. Following God in the absurd has an aha at the end of the road.

Beth Moore was willing to be thought a fool that day, willing to risk losing her social dignity. What about you? What would you have done? Maybe stare at the old man like everyone else? Or maybe create reasons to justify your silence as you sat in your seat? Beth simply chose to obey God's odd command. And because she did, some people that

> We are all called to be fools for Christ. Holy fools.

day saw a reflection of Christ. All because one woman was willing to play the fool.[22]

In reality, we are all called to be fools for Christ. Holy fools. And this involves more than just "standing up for what you believe" in an ungodly culture. Any religious person can do that. But for a Christ-lover, it sometimes means choosing to obey God and show love when those around us are unwilling or incapable of doing so.

So what's the point of God asking us to appear foolish? Won't that just make people laugh at us? And won't that hinder rather than help the cause of Christ?

Maybe. But maybe not. It's not our responsibility to control people's response to our obedience. Our responsibility is only to "trust and obey." God may never ask you to publically brush an old man's hair. It's more likely He will ask you to love your spouse when your friends are bailing on their marriages. Or to give up some social activities so you can spend more time with your children. Or to appear to be a fool by saying no to that job promotion because it meant you'd have to move and leave your church family.

> More than anything, you seek to live life closer to the heart of Jesus, sensitive to His Spirit's promptings in you.

Or it could mean showing kindness and acceptance to that odd-looking person who walks into your church this Sunday. But what it means more than anything is that you seek to live life closer to the heart of Jesus, sensitive to His Spirit's promptings in you. And being willing to obey even though it may sound unconventional or out of the ordinary…even to your Christian friends.

Fifth-Gospel Christians aren't weird so they can draw attention to themselves. They don't act different in order to feel better about themselves. But when God clearly leads them, they obey. They care more what God thinks about them than what others may think. And by doing so, they prove themselves just crazy enough to believe God might use them to change the world.

GOSPEL APPEALS

- *God distinguishes His followers by inviting them into the ridiculous.*
- *Following God in the ridiculous may produce critics on the front end, but it may also draw converts on the back end.*
- *Remember Paul's words: "For the message of the cross is foolishness to those who are perishing" (1 Corinthians 1:18 NIV).*

Questions for Further Thought and Discussion

1. It turns out that living the ridiculous actually has a purpose. Can you share a time in your life when God asked you to do the seemingly absurd?

2. Critics of Scripture often point out the apparent ridiculous in the Bible as a reason not to believe. How can this chapter help you better explain some of the reasoning behind God's odd ways?

3. Is God asking something ridiculous of you at this time in your life?

4. There's a danger in trying to make sense of everything before you follow God. What is the danger?

5. Does following God in the ridiculous work contrary to wisdom or should the Christian embrace both? Explain.

6. What is your biggest takeaway from this chapter?

Chapter 8

WEAK IS THE NEW STRONG

"All God's giants have been weak men who did great things for God because they reckoned on God being with them."

Hudson Taylor

To some people, Christianity is a faith full of apparent contradictions. Paradoxes. Stuff that doesn't seem to mesh. Things that don't make a whole lot of sense upon first, and sometimes second, glance. Things like:

- Love your enemies.
- The way to be exalted is to be humble.
- To truly live you have to die.
- Jesus gave His life, not for good people but for sinful, ungodly people who don't deserve it.

Okay, so here's another one for you.

- To be strong, you have to be very weak.

Wait, that doesn't make sense. By definition, if you're weak, then you're *not* strong, right? And if you're weak, you're just...well, *weak*. So how can strength possibly be found in weakness?

Similarly, when was the last time you heard someone exclaim, "Being weak is rad!"? That's like being deep in debt, desperately needing cash, and yet singing the praises of poverty. There's something not right about that.

It would appear that there's no room in our culture for this scriptural value of "weakness."

Weakness is not a value in our culture. We Americans pride ourselves on being self-made, independent, resilient...and *strong*. If you surveyed the American populace and asked, "What are the top ten American values?," weakness wouldn't come close to making the list. That's because weakness is perceived as a limitation. A liability. Almost like a social disease. Weak people are looked down upon. They're considered losers. In a world obsessed with the survival of the fittest, it would appear that there's no room in our culture for this scriptural value of "weakness."

Thanks a lot, God.

But could there be more to this than meets the eye? Something beneath the surface? Something deeper? Something beneficial? Even admirable?

Ironically, from God's vantage point, weakness is actually one of His favorite qualities. But why? And how? Doesn't this continue to promote the reputation of Christians as passive *wimps*? Possibly. But it all depends on your perspective and definition of *weakness*.

Cinderella Stories

Every spring, the sporting world pauses to watch the entertaining, adrenaline-generating spectacle known as the NCAA Basketball Tournament (women, bear with me for a second). Known as "March Madness," it dominates TV ratings. Keep in mind, I live in a state that is home to both Duke University and the University of North Carolina, two college basketball giants. (We have jokes here about God loving UNC so much He made the sky Tar-Heel blue.) Virtually every year those two teams are in the tournament.

But one thing about March Madness is that you can always count on at least one Cinderella story—a team that, despite the odds, somehow manages to keep on winning. They usually end up becoming a crowd favorite. Millions of fans momentarily forget the perennial powerhouses and find themselves instead cheering for some obscure school from Nowheresville. And it's one reason why we keep watching every year.

I've come to believe that God loves the underdog.

As I read my Bible, I've come to believe that God loves the underdog. He loves it when people are told to give it up, to hang up the cleats, to throw in the towel because they have no conceivable chance of winning. He delights in a David who can't even suit up for battle because he's not big enough to wear soldier's armor. The nerve of a little shepherd boy thinking he can slay the world's most intimidating giant.

Or imagine you're launching a worldwide ministry. Would you choose a bunch of smelly redneck fishermen, a cheating tax collector with a horrible reputation, a political assassin, and a few cocky braggarts? Of course not. But Jesus did.

Everyone (and I mean everyone) told Sarah she would never have a child. Even *she* didn't believe it. But at the ripe old age of ninety-one, here comes Isaac, the promised son.

Many thought that youth was a huge disadvantage for novice missionary-ministers like John Mark and Timothy, but apparently God was just getting started with them. They were nobodies with no chance of success. Or so people thought.

God seems to enjoy working against all odds. He likes it when people bet against the weak one. He laughs when people fail to see the value and potential in His children. It's usually about this time that He steps in, as if to say, "Watch this." And all of heaven stands to cheer. Applauding for the underdog, the spiritual equivalent of the Cinderella story.

Cracked Pots

So what exactly is it about our weakness that God loves so much? Why is this such a value to Him?

To begin with, when we're weak, we usually know it, and that puts us in a position to be used by God. Abraham Lincoln said, "God must love the common man, He made so many of them." And a common, weak person in the hand of an all-powerful God has far more potential than a strong person who lives independently of Him. From God's perspective weakness is not a limitation but a divine opportunity for us to partner with Him. To give us *His* strength.

Imagine if we could see our weaknesses as opportunities for God to use us. To even see our impotence and imperfections as our *witness*. Sound strange? Maybe so, but what if weaknesses cease to be limitations when we offer them up to an unlimited God. Let your mind soak in the words of Isaiah,

> He gives *strength* to the *weary*
>   and increases the *power* of the *weak*.
> Even youths grow *tired* and *weary*,
>   and young men *stumble* and *fall*;
> but those who hope in the LORD
>   will renew their *strength*.
> They will *soar* on wings like eagles;
>   they will *run* and *not grow weary*,
>   they will *walk* and *not be faint*.[1]

Our God loves pouring His strength into weak people, even using those weaknesses for His glory.

But sometimes the very weakness we lament is the very thing God wants to use for His glory. In Paul's second letter to the Corinthians, he helps us see the importance of embracing weakness: "But we have this treasure in jars of clay, to show that the surpassing

Sometimes the very weakness we lament is the very thing God wants to use for His glory.

power belongs to God and not to us."[2] Paul is contrasting his weakened state with the surpassing power at work within him.

But what is "this treasure" and what are the "jars of clay"? First, the treasure refers to the Gospel—the Good News of Jesus Christ as contained in the New Covenant. It's the beautiful Gospel that brings hope, help, and eventually heaven. Second, jars of clay refers to our frail human bodies. Paul's figurative language demonstrates how our bodies, like jars of clay, are fragile, flawed, weak, and limited.

These jars or clay pots in Paul's day were inexpensive, easily broken, and easily replaceable. They were expendable. People often hid their valuables (such as silver or gold) in these clay pots. And here is where Paul makes his point. What made these common jars of clay valuable was the treasure contained *within* them.

In 1947, the famous Dead Sea Scrolls were discovered when a shepherd boy in the Qumran community threw a stone into a cave and heard the sound of something breaking. Running quickly toward the sound, he discovered what later proved to be a treasure trove of ancient biblical manuscripts. And yet, this treasure was encased in pots made of ordinary clay.

As Christians, though we are weak, we carry within us a great treasure for the world. Though it is often disguised, we nevertheless have it inside us. We are walking God-containers—carrying the greatest treasure of all time—the good news of salvation through Jesus.

But the truth is, we're all weak in some way. We're all disposable. All of us have limitations. We're like those jars of clay. The only difference between the world and us is we are jars with God's treasure inside. The world is full of empty clay jars and the church is full of treasure-filled jars. Sadly this treasure is often hidden, stored away like Thanksgiving china, out of sight of those who so desperately need it.

The weaker we become, the greater God's power is released in our lives.

"But," you may wonder, "why did God put such an amazing treasure in ordinary, common clay pots?" Answer: To put His grace and greatness on display. Here's the deal: *The weaker we become, the greater God's power is released in our lives.*

Talk about paradox. As commentator David Garland wrote, God does this "to show that the treasure has nothing to do with the pot."[3] Our weakness highlights God's strength. Our insignificance showcases His greatness. God is not looking for our strength but for weakness. God doesn't need strength. He's got plenty of that. The weaker we are, the greater God's power can flow through our lives. Isn't that exciting!

"Aha," you say. "Now it's beginning to make sense why God allowed me to be weak in (fill in the blank here)." And the good news is that we're never too weak to be used by God.

I'll admit it. I'm weak. Very weak. Considering my limitations, I'm humbled that God would ever use me. I'm thankful that God's not interested in my strengths—which aren't many anyway. He's interested in my weakness.

When I came to Christ at the age of nineteen, I was totally uneducated. The only book I remember reading growing up was a children's book called *Freckle Juice* by Judy Blume. I cheated my way through high school (and now you know). Following high school, I wanted to join the Marine Corps. To get in, I needed at least a 31 on the Armed Services Vocational Aptitude Battery (ASVAB), a required test for everyone going into the military. Well, I failed...abysmally. I had to wait thirty days, and then I failed it again. I was humiliated. So I waited six months...and yes, I failed it again. I couldn't even be a jarhead because apparently I was an empty head. Then I found out the US Army would take a score of 28, so I took the test again. I scored a 27.

Anyone who knew me back in high school knew I wasn't the brightest bulb on campus.

Loser.

Thankfully, the army gave me a waiver, but then I failed the physical. Are you believing this? I mean, could I be any weaker? I felt so dense and ill-equipped. I was *that* senior sitting in class with sophomores. Anyone who knew me back in high school knew I wasn't the brightest bulb on campus. I wasn't articulate. I had a poor vocabulary and couldn't type to save my life.

Then, after becoming a Christian, I fell in love with Jesus. I started memorizing Scripture, and all I wanted to do was talk about the treasure residing within this uneducated, common clay pot.

At the Ritz Carlton, in Dana Point, California, where I worked, they nicknamed me "the Reverend." Quite the contrast from my party-boy, drug-using, alcohol-filled, promiscuous past. Eventually, people began saying, "Bobby, I could see you in full-time ministry." They were starting to see God's strength in my weakness.

I enrolled in Bible college. My grades were decent, but it was difficult academically. I decided to go on to seminary, so I painstakingly taught myself to type. While in seminary, I was embarrassed to have my laptop open because I typed so slowly. But by the time I graduated from Dallas Seminary, I could type with the best of them. My grades had improved dramatically.

Boosted with confidence, I began my doctoral studies in apologetics, and I graduated with highest honors—summa cum laude. And today, I'm working on my second doctorate, a PhD in the philosophy of religion at the University of Birmingham in England. Call it my own Cinderella story.

> God releases His power into our weaknesses so other people can see the treasure residing within these clay pots.

So how did all this happen? How did an uneducated party boy go from being an academic pauper and army flunky to earning a doctorate? Was it because of something great in me? Yes. But it was nothing in and of myself. It was God's great strength and treasure at work in and through me. The Gospel was changing my life and mind, God's power making up for my lost time.

It amazes me to think I'm sitting here writing this book, that I serve as a pastor, speak across the country, and have a global apologetics ministry. My testimony is actually "bragimony" of God's grace. The simple fact is that He took my weaknesses, my past, my sin, and even my stupidity, and used it for His glory. That's what God does *so well*. He releases His power into our weaknesses so other people can see the treasure residing within these old, cracked clay pots.

You may think, *Well, my pot isn't just cracked. It's completely broken.* But God puts the pieces back together so that His light is released through the remaining cracks. When a vessel falls and breaks open, all the observers can see the goods within. When we recognize our brokenness, God's light and truth is released for all to see. He shines through *broken* weakness.

So it's not enough to be weak. We also have to surrender our brokenness to God. Broken Christians release God's power in and through their lives. God wants us spilling the Gospel treasure from our cracked pots into the treasure-seeking world around us. Only as our pots are cracked can the light of the true treasure inside spring forth.

Paul knew all this. He knew God's truth and his own culture. He was a missionally urgent man with a timeless message that *weak is the new strong.*[4] Paul knew that Christians who surrender their weaknesses to God make much of God and glorify Him.

Assessing Your Weaknesses

We all have weaknesses and limitations. That's par for the course for mere jars of clay. As humans we are finite, limited, imperfect. Even sinful. However, when it comes to weaknesses, we don't all share the same ones. There are different types of weaknesses with varying degrees of limitations.

Physical Weaknesses

We know that Paul had a particular physical weakness. He called it his "thorn in the flesh."[5] We aren't completely sure what he meant by this description. Some have suggested that it referred to poor eyesight, which he did suffer from. But there are other, equally valid opinions as well, though none conclusive. What we do know is that Paul's thorn arrived after he had been given some spectacular visions from God. He writes:

> So to keep me from becoming conceited because of the surpassing greatness of the revelations, a thorn was given me in the flesh, a messenger of Satan to harass me, to keep me from becoming conceited. Three times I pleaded with the Lord about this, that it should leave me. But he said to me, "My grace is sufficient for you, for my power is made perfect in weakness." Therefore I will boast all the more gladly of my weaknesses, so that the power of Christ may rest upon me. For the sake of Christ, then, I am content with weaknesses, insults, hardships, persecutions, and calamities. For when I am weak, then I am strong.[6]

What can we learn about Paul's thorn? First, this thorn was a physical limitation—"in the flesh." Second, it was designed to keep him humble. Knowing human nature as He does, God was aware of man's natural tendency to become proud, especially after being given special, secret revelation from God Almighty.

Pride is a powerful drug, poisoning virtually everything else about us. It was the root of Lucifer's rebellion and is one of the sins God especially hates.[7] So God is especially concerned that this wickedness not take root in Paul's heart. The apostle had been chosen to be God's primary mouthpiece for spreading the Gospel to the Gentiles. Pride would be a strategic way Satan (and Paul's own sin nature) could ensnare him. So God gave him something to remind him that he was still just an ordinary man.

But this mysterious thorn also enabled Paul to become a greater witness. It meant he could identify with others who had limitations. Of course, that didn't mean Paul was happy about it, and on three separate occasions he begged God to take it away. And how did God respond? By removing the thorn? By making him comfortable and pain-free? Nope. God told him, "My grace will be enough for you." And what's the point of that? Because His power is best displayed in our weakness.

That can be a hard pill for American Christians to swallow. We prefer comfort and a storm-free faith. Our initial response to the first sign of pain or limitation is, "I've got to get rid of this." And yet, God doesn't usually go there. He doesn't think like we do. God's plan for Paul was to create a unique dependence on Him. And this strength proved to be greater than what Paul could've achieved in the thorn's absence.

Another divine paradox.

Paul would certainly need this great strength as a pioneer missionary and church planter. He would require a special strength to sustain him through the intense perils and pressures he would experience.[8] God was essentially saying to Paul, "Son, I am enough."

So how does Paul respond? He eventually comes to a place where, instead of pestering God about his weaknesses, he embraces them. He submits to God's higher power, wisdom, and ways. I like that about Paul. He knew when to quit praying and complaining and just get on with the business of living.

Some may say, "Never quit praying for relief. Never quit praying for that miracle." But Paul would disagree. He stopped praying after three intense sessions with the Lord. But how can you know when to stop praying for God to remove a physical weakness? When God says to you, "My grace is sufficient for you." This acceptance of God's plan inspired Paul to declare, "Therefore, I will boast all the more *gladly* of my weaknesses, so that the power of Christ may rest upon me." He went from praying in agony for God to get rid of his physical weakness to boasting gladly in his weakness.

What a change. "It's great being weak," Paul claims. And how was he able to do this? Because he realized it's better to have Christ's power rest upon him than it is to be proud and live independent of Him. Paul learned the simple, deep, and powerful truth that *God is enough*.

Is He enough for you? *Is* He? Even in your greatest and most debilitating weakness and limitations? What if your physical circumstances never change this side of heaven? Have you come to a place in your life where you honestly believe, "God is enough"?

After I became a Christian, the first church I joined was Saddleback Church where Rick Warren serves as senior pastor. As a new Christian, I had no idea how to pick a church. I just knew there was a big church that met in a tent (at the time) that had a ministry called "Celebrate Recovery," which helped people overcome their hurts, habits, and hang ups.

Once I became a member at Saddleback, I learned that Rick suffers from a strange adrenaline allergy. This can be an incredible challenge for him, especially as a public communicator. Anyone who speaks publicly knows that adrenaline and speaking are like ball and glove—they go together. Rick has to remain totally calm before speaking or this adrenaline can kick in, causing him to lose his sight. There have been times when he's teaching that he cannot see his audience. Imagine that. So he developed a secret cue: if he wipes his forehead with his forearm it means he needs prayer because he can't see the audience. Rick Warren, megachurch pastor and best-selling author, communicating the good news out of *weakness*.

Be encouraged, Christian. As long as you are breathing, God is still at work in you. He's not finished with you yet.[9] You can be blind, on your deathbed, handicapped, paralyzed, or suffer from chronic migraines, and God can still use you. You can have cancer, HIV, heart disease, psoriasis, autism, and fibromyalgia—but as long as you are alive, God can cause your life to impact others.

Truth is, we are weak from the time we exit our mother's womb. Every rose has its thorn, but thorns don't have to stop us from being used by God. Paul had his thorn. Rick Warren has his. Jacob had his limp. And you have yours. We all do.

Intellectual Weaknesses

I'm thankful that one doesn't have to be an Einstein to be used in God's kingdom work. God uses both the intellectually elite and the intellectually challenged who trust in Him.[10] However, know this. You may not be formally educated, but if you know God and His Word, you can have more wisdom than someone with multiple degrees to his name.[11] God's wisdom always trumps worldly knowledge. And we have the mind of Christ.[12]

Emotional Weaknesses

Some people seem like robots, devoid of human emotions. Like Mr. Spock from *Star Trek*, they're stoic. Reticent. Aloof. For most, that's just their personality. For others, certain tragic experiences in the past may cause them to be emotionally paralyzed. On the other end of the spectrum, some tend to *over* emote, wearing their feelings on their sleeve.

We run to medication like euphoric twelve-year-old girls toward a Justin Bieber concert.

Today, more people are on emotional quieting pills than ever before as they struggle with anxieties, depression, PMS, insecurities, worries, fears, and anger. Though chemical treatment can often help regulate certain physiological imbalances, ours has become a nation that is *way* overmedicated. We run to medication like euphoric twelve-year-old girls toward a Justin Bieber concert. We are overly dependent on drugs to give us the emotional stability we need.

Because sin affects every part of us—physical, mental, intellectual, and emotional—our feelings are naturally unstable, often swinging from one extreme to another. Often they control us, determining our mood and greatly impacting our relationships. At worst, they can control most everything about us. At best, they cannot be fully trusted. They can, and often do, deceive and mislead us, causing us to believe things that are not true. They also inform our choices, which is what affects virtually every part of our lives.

An *angry* person may learn to control angry outbursts but still experience a constant low-level amount of anger. I've come to believe that many visionaries struggle from *anxiety* because they live so much in the future, seeking to solve problems that may never come to fruition. Yet, the older and more mature one gets, the less this emotion will rule one's life.

> Christ alone, not our emotions, must dominate us.

But here is a reality: Christians do not have to be dominated by these emotional weaknesses. We can learn to submit our emotional struggles to Christ. He alone, not our emotions, must dominate us. And when this happens over time, we find that our emotions become more balanced and healthy, serving us properly. In this way emotions are a wonderful thing, and we have so many things to properly be emotional about as believers, from excitement, enthusiasm, celebration, anticipation, and even godly anger. As long as they *follow* and do not *lead*. Emotions make great servants but cruel and horrible masters.

Relational Weaknesses

You've probably heard the expression "socially awkward." That's just another way of saying "relationally weak." Just as there are physical, intellectual, and emotional weaknesses, there are also relational weaknesses. Some people are especially gifted in the relational department. However, some preachers and public personalities I've known struggle with relating to others. And this can be very challenging and frustrating, though God can still use them. They just need to recognize their weakness and trust God to strengthen them through it.

I can't know this for certain, but John the Baptist strikes me as a socially awkward dude. He obviously struggled with fashion issues, having one outfit in his closet—a camel-hair garment, a pair of sandals, and an old belt. His diet weirds me out too—devouring locusts and wild honey. And he *was* a bit of a loner, hanging out in the wilderness and along the Jordan River. Nevertheless, no one would argue that God didn't use him in amazing ways. Picture John on a Christian TV talk show. Never mind.

Here was a guy with a really serious message, yelling at people that God's judgment was about to fall. Yet when it came time for Jesus to be baptized, He went straight to John. Talk about a ministry opportunity. God took what many would see as a relational weakness and turned it into something great for His glory. He can do the same for you.

Spiritual Weaknesses

As humans, we are both physical and spiritual beings, and while we may not be able to relate to all the other weaknesses, we all find common ground in our spiritual limitations. We are all guilty sinners until we come to the cross for cleansing. And yet, even then, we still continue to struggle with sin. But God is excellent at taking sinners like us and using us in His kingdom work. If you think about it, that's really all He has to work with.

So what about you? What will you do if:

- You lose your main source of income and wonder how you're going to make ends meet?
- Your husband has to relocate for a new job and you don't want to go?
- A loved one dies unexpectedly?
- Your dream business shatters right before your eyes?
- You find out you have terminal cancer?

Will God be enough for you during those times? Is He enough to sustain you in the problems and irritations of daily life?

And what's your excuse for why God can't use you in a great way, in spite of your weakness?

Do you battle with the flesh and reoccurring sin—like Samson or Peter?

Do you struggle with emotional issues—like David?

Do you have a problem with pride—like James or John?

Do social relationships sometimes paralyze or frustrate you—like they did Paul or Timothy?

Do you feel too uneducated or unqualified to be an effective witness for God—like shepherd Amos or fisherman Andrew?

Do you have physical limitations you feel prevent you from being a powerful light for God's kingdom work—like Paul or Moses?

We began this chapter talking about the amazing paradoxes of the Christian faith. But of all those apparent contradictions and often-confusing truths, perhaps the most extraordinary one of them all is *you*.

To think that God could and would use a redeemed sinner like you with all your baggage, past and present hurts, hang-ups, and struggles—all your limitations and weaknesses. And yet He still wants to shine through you, His glorious light beaming through the cracks in your clay pot. *His* strength in *your* weakness. His *grace* as your *sufficiency*.

Now *that* is something worth smiling about.

GOSPEL APPEALS

- *Cracked pots expose more light.*
- *The weaker you become, the more God's power is released in your life.*
- *Human weakness in the hands of the Almighty ceases to be weakness.*

Questions for Further Thought and Discussion

1. How does our culture's view of weakness make it harder for us to embrace our weaknesses?

2. We spend more time trying to cover up our weaknesses than we do exposing them. Why is it important to be more authentic about real weaknesses?

3. Let's get real. Are you trying to hide a weakness that perhaps God wants to use?

4. Can you remember a time when God met you in weakness? If you're going through these questions in a small group, tell the other members about it.

5. Why must we be careful to not place value on people according to their strengths? What can potentially happen to a culture that does this?

6. How can God's love for the weak be a great source of encouragement for the many lost people who consider themselves "the least of these"?

Chapter 9

THE ULTIMATE TRUMP CARD

"Do not waste your time bothering whether you 'love' your neighbor: Act as if you did."

C.S. LEWIS

"The greatest of these is love."

PAUL THE APOSTLE

In his biography, the late Steve Jobs describes his love for the music of Yo-Yo Ma, the great classical cellist. Jobs was such a fan that he invited Yo-Yo Ma to play at a dinner event for the Apple entrepreneur. With his 1712 Stradivarius cello in hand, the musician wowed Jobs and his guests. So touched was Jobs that afterward he said, "You playing Bach on the cello is the best argument I've ever heard for the existence of God, because I don't really believe a human being alone can do this."[1] Later, after Steve Jobs was diagnosed with cancer, he made Ma promise to play at his funeral—a promise Ma would deliver on. For Jobs the music of Ma pointed beyond the cellist to a Creator.

Though Jobs was a Buddhist and as far as we know did not acknowledge the true God, his point is nevertheless legit. Who can doubt the beauty of music? Music speaks. It's a language of its own. Music played beautifully does indeed point beyond the musician.

However, two thousand years ago, the Lord Jesus Christ told His disciples about a better way to convince the world of God's reality. He simply said, "By this all people will know that you are my disciples, if you have love for one another."[2]

Love.

Could something as simple as love be enough to persuade sinful hearts? Is love really the music the world is waiting to hear? The late Francis Schaeffer claimed, "Love is the final apologetic." But exactly how could love be such a powerful tool for reaching nonbelievers? In what way is love the greatest answer to a confused and chaotic world?

A More Excellent Way

Early in my ministry, I was invited to Clinton, Arkansas, to preach in a little Baptist church. Upon arriving, my wife and I went inside and found a seat in one of the pews. I was unprepared for what happened next.

An elderly lady came up to me and said, "Excuse me, you are in my seat."

I was stunned. Speechless. Did I really hear her say that? She just stood there with this deadpan look, waiting for me to get up and move. I felt like telling her to take a hike, but God somehow gave me the grace to keep my mouth shut.

My wife and I moved to the next row, a little nervous that someone else was going to give us the boot. After we sang a few songs, I was introduced and proceeded to deliver my message.

Afterward, the elderly lady approached me and said, "I am sorry about asking you to get out of my seat. I had no idea you were the guest speaker."

I said, "Ma'am, with all due respect, I am a Christian. I can handle it. But if I were a nonbeliever and I came to visit this church and you did that to me, I would never come back again." I then quietly walked away.

This kind of attitude repulses nonbelievers. Love draws people near, but self-love drives people away. According to Jesus, love is a visual, tangible witness to the wonder of God Himself. And the church is where love is to be experienced in spades. Yet, sometimes it's the one thing missing.

> The church is where love is to be experienced in spades. Yet, sometimes it's the one thing missing.

The greatest treatise on love ever written is found in 1 Corinthians 13. The apostle Paul was writing to a group of believers who had lost sight of being Fifth-Gospel Christians. The Corinthian church was a royal mess—inept at love, filled with division, abusing spiritual gifts, gossiping, competitive...you name it. If you ever feel like your church is in bad shape, read 1 Corinthians.

By chapter 13 Paul has brought several accusations against the Corinthians, and now he offers up the great antidote for unifying their church. After discussing the role of spiritual gifts, he lets them know how they can truly impact each other. He says, "And I will show you still a more excellent way to exercise these spiritual gifts of yours. Something even better than the gifts themselves."[3] This *excellent way* of life is...*love*.

> If I speak in the tongues of men and of angels, but have not love, I am a noisy gong or a clanging cymbal. And if I have prophetic powers, and understand all mysteries and all knowledge, and if I have all faith, so as to remove mountains, but have not love, I am nothing. If I give away all I have, and if I deliver up my body to be burned, but have not love, I gain nothing.[4]

In one short paragraph, Paul brushstrokes a beautiful portrait for us. He wants the Corinthians (and us) to know that gifts minus love are worthless and empty. And *words are not enough*: "If I speak in the tongues of men and of angels, but have not love, I am a noisy gong or a clanging cymbal." Paul goes on to say, prophetic powers are not enough. Understanding mysteries is not enough. Knowledge is not enough. Even faith is not enough. Moreover, generosity and even sacrificing for God is nothing compared to the beauty of love.

This was a radical paradigm shift for the Corinthian believers. They had enthusiastically welcomed the gifts and the exercise of the supernatural. They were really into the spectacular. They were wowed by the amazing power displayed through prophecy and truth. They enjoyed the knowledge of God. But all this knowledge did was make them proud.[5] Their power and giftedness without love only fed their sinful nature, inflating their egos. This highly gifted church desperately needed to be filled with God's relentless, unconditional love.

Nobody is going to know you are Jesus' disciples by your giftedness.

Paul is saying, "You can have great faith and stellar Bible studies. You can experience miracles and even die for Jesus. But without this one quality, you are nothing. You guys are like an orchestra of cymbals. A band of gongs. Noisy, but noneffective. And the sound you're making causes people to cover their ears and walk away. That's counterproductive. Nobody is going to know you are Jesus' disciples by your giftedness. Being good, talented, and even professional won't cut it with God. It falls sort. It's not enough."

But *love is enough*. Without love the church fails to please God's heart. You can be a church with few gifts, but if you are abundant in love, you can reach others for Christ. Love is the ultimate trump card, the most important and powerful asset you possess.

Let Me Count the Ways

But Paul isn't finished. He now gets more specific, defining in the next few verses exactly what this kind of love looks like. Unfortunately, in the English language we have only one word for love and it's…are you ready…it's the word *love*. Our language is limited this way. We *love* ice cream. We *love* our favorite football team. And we *love* Jesus. Same word but *vastly* different meanings.

But the Greek language employs different words to describe different types of love. For example, there's *eros*, which refers to sexual love. There's *phileo*, which is brotherly love. But when Paul wants to describe the highest and greatest love of all, he uses a unique word—*agape*. This word describes a love without conditions. Not "I love you *when*…," "I love you *if*…," or "I love you *because*…," but simply "I choose to love you." Period. The end. And for always.

Agape is a love without strings attached. A love without limits. Without borders. It's the kind of love found in John 3:16, "God so loved the world, that he gave his only Son, that whoever believes in him should not perish but have eternal life." It's a demonstrable love. It's the love of Romans 5:8, "But God *shows* his love for us in that while we were still sinners, Christ died for us." But let's get even more specific and personal. Paul now takes a black-and-white word and infuses it with color. He writes to his Corinthian friends:

> *Agape* is a love without strings attached. A love without limits.

> Love is patient and kind; love does not envy or boast; it is not arrogant or rude. It does not insist on its own way; it is not irritable or resentful; it does not rejoice at wrongdoing, but rejoices with the truth. Love bears all things, believes all things, hopes all things, endures all things.
>
> Love never ends.[6]

Okay, that's a really high standard. So how do I apply this to my life? Good question. I'll give you the same test that was once given to me. (*Warning*: This may sting a little…or perhaps a lot.) Take the above passage and replace the words *love* and *it* with your name. For example,

> *Bobby* is patient and kind; *Bobby* does not envy or boast;
> *he* is not arrogant or rude. *He* does not insist on his own
> way [yeah right]; *he* is not irritable or resentful [no, not
> at all]; *he* does not rejoice at wrongdoing, but rejoices
> with the truth. *Bobby* bears all things, believes all things,
> hopes all things, endures all things.
>
> *Bobby* never ends [or fails].

Okay, that was awkward. If you knew me, you'd be thinking, *Yeah, that brother could use some work in the love department.* I've done this exercise more than once, and I always immediately see where I need to grow. So go ahead, try it on yourself. Take a minute and insert your name, reading it out loud if you can.

How'd you do? Pretty revealing, isn't it. Now let's both do another test, one that lets us see love in living color. This time, replace the word *love* with *Jesus.*

> Jesus is patient and kind; Jesus does not envy or boast;
> He is not arrogant or rude. He does not insist on His
> own way; He is not irritable or resentful; He does not
> rejoice at wrongdoing, but rejoices with the truth. Jesus
> bears all things, believes all things, hopes all things,
> endures all things.
>
> Jesus never ends.

Jesus Christ is
love in action.
He's our model.
He's the one
we're trying to
show the world.

Ah, now it fits. So refreshing to read it that way, isn't it? It felt right. Appropriate. And it also reveals just how far we have to go in becoming like our Master and Savior. At the same time though, it fills us with comfort and hope, knowing that our God and best friend perfectly incarnates this love. He *defines* love. He *is* love. Jesus Christ is love in action. He's our model. He's the one we're trying to show the world. He is the First Gospel that we Fifth-Gospel Christians are seeking to emulate. He's our measure. Our standard. The One we must reflect.

Yes, Jesus is the Gospel. He's the Good News the world needs. When the world sees Christ in Christians, they just might want our Christ. A Fifth-Gospel Christian seeks to reflect Christ so the world can know His love as we do. We live a life of love so they can experience God's endless love too.

Picture in your mind a church that is patient. A truly kind church. One that doesn't envy other churches or boast about their own accomplishments. Imagine a church that is not arrogant or rude to visitors or people who aren't like they are. A church that doesn't insist on its own way. A church that's not irritable or resentful.

Are you seeing it? It isn't hard at all to imagine a church like that making an impact on the world. We've got to get away from our romanticized view of love. Love is much more than a feeling. It's a *verb*. An "action noun." Love is a personal decision we make each day. It's a choice we make to love one another in the body of Christ. Only with Christ's *agape* love can we love the unlovely, the unloving, and the unlovable.

> Only with Christ's *agape* love can we love the unlovely, the unloving, and the unlovable.

Love Hurts

According to Jesus, love is the great distinguisher. It's what makes the difference. Through His earthly mission, He raised the love standard for the church. He told His disciples, "A new command I give you: Love one another. As I have loved you, so you must love one another. By this everyone will know that you are my disciples, if you love one another."[7]

It would have been much easier had He just reminded us of the Ten Commandments and left it at that. "Now while I'm gone, you guys don't kill each other and lie and stuff like that." That sounds a whole lot easier than "love each other in the *same way* I have loved you."

"Oh, is that all, Jesus? Sure. Consider it done."

Not.

We find the Lord's request (*command* actually) a wee bit intimidating, don't we? Even the spirit behind the Ten Commandments is to "love your neighbor as yourself,"[8] but Jesus spells it out for us here in bold caps and red letters.

L-O-V-E O-N-E A-N-O-T-H-E-R.

Love that person who rubs you the wrong way. Love the unfaithful. The immature. The obnoxious teenager. The grumpy father-in-law. The noisy neighbor. The *nosey* neighbor. The fruitcake-making aunt. The unfair boss. The inconsistent friend. The lazy worker. The worrying wife. The hateful husband. The wannabe hipster. The argumentative church member. The unruly two-year-old. The angry atheist. The bitter, unattractive single woman. The unwise college student. The blatant homosexual. That snippy sister-in-law. The Muslim.

"Love them," Jesus says. "No, really. Show them who I really am by bringing some *agape* their way."

Isn't that what Jesus did for us? He loved us with His whole life. And in His death. His love is sacrificial and selfless. To really love someone means you are willing to give your life for them if that's what it takes. We must do *whatever* is necessary to love each other. Granted, most of us won't literally die showing love for someone, but we all must be willing to sacrifice while we live.

How would your church be different if its members loved like this? What problems could be solved? What lives would be saved? And what is the ultimate outcome of this kind of love? "All people will know that you are my disciples."

Our *people*-loving flows out of our *God*-loving.

Ah, our love gives evidence not only of our discipleship but of Jesus' existence. And our *people*-loving flows out of our *God*-loving. Jesus has given us a teaching that walks. It's meant to be lived. Many years ago, we sang a song in Christian circles. Looking back, the melody is pretty cheesy and dated, but the title still rings true: "They'll Know We Are Christians by Our Love."

Love is the signature of every genuine believer in Jesus. It's a love on display for all the world to see. Again, the words of Francis Shaeffer challenge Jesus' church,

> Upon his authority he gives the world the right to judge whether you or I are born-again Christians on the basis of our observable love toward all Christians...[If] people come up to us and cast in our teeth the judgment that we are not Christians because we have not shown love toward other Christians, we must understand that they are only exercising a prerogative which Jesus gave them.[9]

Ouch.

Wait a minute, you may be thinking. *Some people are just hard to love.*

I know. Believe me, I know. And Jesus knows it too. But there's something else to remember here. You and I can be hard to love too. We are all fickle followers of Jesus, are we not? Wayward children. As the hymn writer penned, "Prone to wander, Lord, I feel it. Prone to leave the God I love."[10]

If anyone had failed, forsaken, or forgotten us as often as we have failed God, wouldn't we struggle to show them love? But with you and me, God is patient. God is kind.

What a loving God we have.

And that God and His love live in you. *That's* why and how we can love those who are difficult and who get all over our last nerve.

It's easy to love those who love us. In His great Sermon on the Mount, Jesus said,

"You have heard that it was said, 'You shall love your neighbor and hate your enemy.' But I say to you, Love your enemies and pray for those who persecute you, so that you may be sons of your Father who is in heaven. For he makes his sun rise on the evil and on the good, and sends rain on the just and on the unjust. For if you love those who love you, what reward do you have? Do not even the tax collectors do the same?"[11]

In 1653, Rembrandt etched a mesmerizing illustration titled *The Three Crosses.* Through this, the artist leads his onlookers to consider love *personified*—to contemplate their own response to Christ in light of others' reactions.

If you were to gaze at this masterpiece, your attention would be drawn first to the center cross where love is crystallized in the person of Jesus Christ. Then your eyes move outward, and you're met with a host of other reactions to Christ's love. You notice a crowd gathered around the foot of the cross, and observe a host of facial expressions and actions of those involved in crucifying the Son of God. On the bottom portion of the painting some people are running away. A lady, perhaps Mary, has fainted at the bottom right area of the painting. Some pull their hair in grief, while others merely pass by, minding their own business. Soldiers on Roman horseback tend to their duties. Others are weeping. Some kneel in front of the cross.

Rembrandt recognized that he too was guilty of crucifying God's Love Gift.

Finally, your eyes find their way to the edge of the painting. There you catch sight of another figure, practically lost in the shadows. Most art critics argue this is a representation of Rembrandt himself, who recognized through his own sins that he too was guilty of crucifying God's Love Gift.[12]

In light of Jesus' death on the cross, how have you responded? If you want to be a Fifth-Gospel Christian, you first must *be* a

Christian. So *are* you? Are you an active follower of Jesus? Do you believe He died in your place—as your substitute? Do you believe His love covers you and removes your hate? Do you believe His death pays for your sin? If so, you find the very love you're looking for at this cross.

This is the core of Christianity, where love begins. It's where we get a picture of what the rest of our life must look like. It's there where we see that sacrificial love has the greatest power to redeem people. If we are going to reach this world, it will be through *experiencing* and *expressing* sacrificial love.

I can pretty much guarantee that you will never hang on a cross. But I trust the cross is nevertheless a grim yet glorious reminder of your call to be a Fifth-Gospel follower of Jesus. Like Rembrandt's etching, not everyone will be interested in your Christ and His Gospel. Our love for God and one another will elicit different reactions from different people. But better many reactions than none at all, right?

We desperately need a resurrection of radical love in the church today. A love that speaks. A love that draws. A love that touches. A love that changes everything.

> We desperately need a resurrection of radical love in the church today.

It's our ace in the hole.

Our ultimate trump card.

GOSPEL APPEALS

- *"Love is the final apologetic" (Francis Schaeffer).*
- *If you empty the Gospel of love, you empty the Gospel of the Gospel.*
- *Love is the signature of every true believer in Jesus.*

Questions for Further Thought and Discussion

1. Why is it so important for the church to love the world?
2. Do you think the world feels loved by the church? Elaborate.
3. What are some ways the church can do a better job loving the world around it?
4. Read 1 Corinthians 13:4-8 and share where you need to grow in the love department.
5. Can you think of a time when you powerfully experienced God's love through someone else? Explain.
6. Is there someone in your life you find it difficult to love? How can meditating on Jesus' love for you increase your ability to show love to this person?

Chapter 10

SHOW AND TELL

"How are they to believe in him of whom they have never heard?"

PAUL THE APOSTLE

*"Christianity is enshrined in the life, but
it is proclaimed by the lips."*

MICHAEL GREEN

Recently, I took my friend Josh to Donut King. That's right, Donut King, the place where policemen go in the afterlife. It's a donut lover's paradise.

Josh's favorite food is donuts. I think it's actually a food group to him. Anyway, Donut King has this raised, maple-glazed donut that can only be described as "heavenly." It's like biting into maple-flavored snow…only better. It's the kind of sensory experience that imprints in your brain. Call it "memory food."

I wish you could have seen Josh's face as he bit into that donut—eyes rolled back into his head, his mouth exploding with flavor. He quickly confessed it was the best donut he had ever tasted, and that's saying something coming from a donut connoisseur like Josh. We couldn't stop talking about how amazing it was.

Driving back to the church, I said, " Josh, have you noticed we talk about the things we love in life? We see a cool car and say, 'Look at that!' or we eat a gourmet meal and feel compelled to say, 'That was great.'" Then I paused. "Why isn't our delight in Jesus verbalized more?"

Could it be that the reason we're not talking to the world about our Savior is that we aren't delighting in Him?

Could it be that the reason we're not talking to the world about our Savior is that we aren't delighting in Him? Could it be that we don't find Him satisfying enough? The psalmist declared, "Taste and see that the LORD is good."[1] But have we tasted? Have we found in Jesus the all-satisfying passion of our lives?

David also wrote, "Delight yourself in the LORD."[2] But for us, Jesus gets trumped by a donut. The Son of God takes second place to a frosted pastry. I was so excited about Donut King that I wanted my friend to experience it. I couldn't keep my mouth shut about it, so I had to bring him to this delicious place. I wonder how many people I've told about Donut King lately compared to how many I've told about the real King. I also wonder if that makes God sad. C.S. Lewis once wrote:

> We delight to praise what we enjoy because the praise not merely expresses but completes our enjoyment; it is its appointed consummation. It is not out of compliment that lovers keep on telling one another how beautiful they are; the delight is incomplete till it is expressed. It is frustrating to have discovered a new author and not be able to tell anyone how good he is; to come suddenly at the turn of the road, upon some mountain valley of unexpected grandeur and then to have to keep silent because the people with you care for it no more than for a tin can in the ditch; to hear a good joke and find no one to share it with.[3]

I love that phrase "the delight is incomplete till it is expressed."

This is never more true than with Jesus. Jesus' disciples were threatened by the authorities of their day, "You guys need to shut up about your faith already." This prompted Peter to reply, "We cannot help speaking about what we have seen and heard."[4]

A False Dichotomy

There is a wildly popularly (but falsely attributed) statement by Saint Francis of Assisi, the Italian Catholic friar and preacher, who supposedly said, "Preach the Gospel at all times. Use words if necessary." Many Christians have used this as a free pass not to evangelize. But there are a few problems with this.

First, Saint Francis never said it. Nothing in his writings leads us to this quote.[5] To the contrary, he stressed the importance of our words matching our deeds. Second, Francis was widely involved in verbally articulating the Gospel. Far from being muzzled, Francis

> sometimes preached in up to five villages a day, often outdoors. In the country, Francis often spoke from a bale of straw or a granary doorway. In town, he would climb on a box or up steps in a public building. He preached to serfs and their families as well as to the landholders, to merchants, women, clerks, and priests— any who gathered to hear the strange but fiery little preacher from Assisi.[6]

Apparently Francis thought "words were *very* necessary" as he was an open-air preacher.

Third, there is no dichotomy between our words and deeds. God wants Christians to *live* the word and *share* the word. To show *and* tell what they have seen and heard. The first disciples *saw* the resurrected Christ. They *heard* His message. And they could not help but *tell* others about Jesus. Our speaking problem may, in reality be a loving problem. Or a delighting issue.

God wants Christians to *live* the word and *share* the word.

Our incarnation of the Gospel is both visual and verbal. It's not either-or but both-and. God wants audiovisual Christians. Words *and* works. To simply live a good Christian life isn't enough. Though God certainly uses our kind deeds, good works, and godly lifestyle,[7] our lives can communicate only so much information about God. Like creation, our lifestyle can reveal *some* things about our Lord, but there is more to being a witness than merely "being an example." That's important, just incomplete. Paul asked the Roman Christians, "How are they to believe in him of whom they have never heard? And how are they to hear without someone preaching?"[8]

If all we do is live the Gospel, people will think we are merely good, moral people.

By living out the Gospel, we gain *credibility*. By verbalizing the Gospel, we provide *clarity*. If all we do is live the Gospel, people will think we are merely good, moral people. But there are plenty of religious and nonreligious moral people in the world. That's why Jesus said we were to be His witnesses.[9] A witness shows *and* tells. He knew that our highest priorities and passions will eventually make their way out of our mouths. That's how we turn *stranger*hoods into *neighbor*hoods and our marketplaces into mission fields. That's how we live the Gospel *out loud*.

"B-B-B-But I'm Not a Speaker"

According to Jesus (a trustworthy authority on the subject), our problem with evangelism is not so much a disinterested audience as a detached church. The harvest isn't the issue here. There are plenty of lost people who are ready to listen. The problem is a dispassionate, paralyzed church.

Imagine Jesus speaking at your church this Sunday and saying, "The harvest is plentiful, but the laborers are few. Therefore pray earnestly to the Lord of the harvest to send out laborers into his harvest."[10] Then He pauses and asks, "When was the last time you told anyone about Me? Have you ever shared My Gospel with someone?"

At this moment in most churches, you could hear the grass

growing outside. The point is not merely to make people feel guilty but to call the church to "mission up." We talk a lot about the 10-40 Window in missions, that geographic region that has the least access to the Gospel and Christian resources. But what about the 9-5 Window? Are we God's "secret service agents" at our jobs, working undercover so no one knows about our faith? Or could there be other reasons why we're so mute about our Master?

Reasons We Don't Speak Up

Here are a few reasons why we don't speak up. Whatever the obstacle, we must find our way through it. Souls are hanging in the balance, but sadly, we remain paralyzed by:

- *Fear*—"What if they reject me?" "What if I make a fool of myself?"

- *Ignorance* (lack of knowledge)—"What if I can't answer their questions?" "What if they shake up my own faith?" "I don't know what to say."

- *Isolation* (no nonbelieving friends)—"Uh, I don't know any non-Christians." "I'm too busy with church and Christian things."

- *Hypocrisy*—"No one who really knows me would ever believe Jesus is real."

- *Apathy*—"I'm really busy." "I don't feel like it." "I just don't care enough to share with them."

How sad that our hearts don't break over the conditions of the lost. Jesus' did.[11] Paul's did. His burden for his fellow Jews was so big that he was willing to go to hell for them if it would have meant they'd go to heaven.[12]

Such a deep burden for nonbelievers is virtually nonexistent today. All fervor is birthed from godly anguish. Here is the great apostle, preacher, and missionary willing to suffer hell for his countrymen. What radical love and compassion. What anguish. And so like his Lord's heart, who *did* suffer God's wrath for us on the cross.

But the good news is that we don't have to go to hell so someone else can go to heaven. We can't. It's impossible. We're not qualified to take hell for them. Jesus already took our punishment.

God wants us to be unashamed of His Son.

Instead, God is asking something much less painful of us. The sacrifice He requires isn't death on a cross, but rather death to our pride and fear of what others might think. God just wants us to be proud of Jesus and what He has done for us. He wants us to be unashamed of His Son. As Paul wrote to Christians surrounded by paganism and immorality, "For I am not ashamed of the gospel, for it is the power of God for salvation to everyone who believes."[13]

What? Me? In the Ministry?

What comes to most Christians' minds when they hear the word *minister* is that man who stands up front on Sunday and preaches. But according to Scripture, God has expanded that definition a bit. The Holy Spirit inspired Paul to write,

> All this is from God, who through Christ reconciled us to himself and gave us the *ministry* of reconciliation; that is, in Christ God was reconciling the world to himself, not counting their trespasses against them, and *entrusting to us* the message of reconciliation. Therefore, we are ambassadors for Christ, God making his appeal through us. We implore you on behalf of Christ, be reconciled to God.[14]

A heart for the lost was what motivated Jesus to come here in the first place. No one was more missionally burdened than He. He was all about reconciliation. Speaking of Himself, Christ said, "For the Son of Man came to seek and to save the lost."[15] That is also the passion He wants us to have, as evidenced in His call to Andrew and Peter, "Follow me, and I will make you fishers of men."[16] In other words, "I will teach you to point others to Me." To live on mission. This is the most meaningful verse in all of Scripture to me. Here's why.

Before being called to ministry, I worked at the Ritz Carlton in Southern California, parking cars as a valet. I had trusted Christ and my life was radically changing. I was living clean and sober with no drugs, alcohol, or promiscuity. The stuff of the past was buried. Jesus and telling others about Him was my top priority.

My nickname at work was "the Reverend." All I wanted to do was talk about Jesus.

I remember getting in trouble at work because the guests were complaining that the valet driver kept changing their radio to K-Wave 107.9, a Christian radio station. As I said before, my nickname at work was "the Reverend." All I wanted to do was talk about Jesus. I couldn't imagine doing anything else. I wanted people to know the Savior who changed me.

Soon, I began wondering if I was supposed to be in full-time ministry. That question was answered once and for all in a parking lot at about 2:00 one morning. I was backing a car into a parking space and noticed the license plate on a car in front of me read "MATT419." For some reason, that plate lit up like a neon light. It was practically glowing. (Not literally, of course, but you get my point.) Of all the cars in the parking lot at 2:00 a.m., that one was parked in front of me. I couldn't shake it. It felt like a message—a personal message—to me from God.

I thought, *What is MATT419? And why do I care?* Then suddenly this thought was impressed on my mind, *Bobby, go look in your Bible at MATT419.* I still remember running through the parking lot, thinking to myself, *God has something for me here.* Finally reaching my Bible, I fumbled through the pages until I found Matthew 4:19. There in plain English, simple enough for a former high-school bonehead to understand, were these words, "Follow me, and I will make you fishers of men."

My jaw literally dropped as my heart burned within me. I was in awe of what was for me a holy moment. Jesus called me to ministry with the same words He called Andrew and Peter. From that point forward I began taking the necessary steps to pursue full-time, vocational ministry. At one point, I was sharing Christ with fifty to a hundred people per week in personal street evangelism. I was that "nut case," standing on a bench or outside the chapel in the open area preaching Jesus at the University of Central Arkansas. I wasn't screaming at people, telling them to "turn or burn." Instead, I was pleading with them to turn to a loving God who could transform their lives.

This passion to tell people about Jesus consumed me. I remember on one occassion I had some down time at work, and I was so burdened to share Jesus that I grabbed a phone book and started calling random strangers, saying, "Hi there, my name is Bobby. I know you don't know me, but Jesus has changed my life so much that I've decided to start calling people to see if they have a relationship with Jesus. Do you mind if I ask you some spiritual questions?" These people thought the same thing you're thinking: "This guy is a freak."

It wasn't the most effective form of outreach, I'll grant you that. But it felt good to be bold, shameless, and passionate about people's souls.

Sometimes I miss that fresh zeal. And in that spirit we must always resist the temptation to *professionalize* our faith, to take something so natural and turn it into a presentation. This makes the Gospel appear artificial. We have to believe that the most loving thing we can do for the world is to share Jesus with them. By contrast, the most *un*loving thing we can do is fail to tell those around us about Jesus.

As I reflect on my youthful evangelistic zeal, I have few, if any, regrets. I was simply being faithful to who I knew and what I knew at the time. I was simply one beggar telling other beggars where to find some bread. I still am.[17]

We have to believe that the most loving thing we can do for the world is to share Jesus with them.

But as I have grown in Christ and His wisdom, I have come to understand that in witnessing, God uses all types of methods and people. There is no magic recipe, and if God leads you to be a bit unorthodox, then be faithful to Him.

However, I've discovered that the majority of people in the culture we live in respond more favorably to the Gospel in the context of *relationships*. People trust people they know more than they do a ranting stranger on the street corner or an unfamiliar voice on the phone.

> People respond more favorably to the Gospel in the context of *relationships*.

Wouldn't you feel more comfortable telling a friend about your Jesus than approaching a random stranger in the mall parking lot? Relationships nurture trust and security. And they tell other people you really care about them. A caring friendship is exponentially more effective than a cold call. But remain sensitive to the Lord. He just may ask you to talk to that stranger in the classroom or airport terminal.

When it comes to helping others "find their voice" in witnessing, there is no shortage of Christian formulas. Again, this can seem so artificial, and I'm not about to add to that list. That would only burden you down with guilt or mislead you into thinking that if you'll just do these four simple steps, you'll be a master evangelist in no time. Not only is that not true, but it trivializes the Gospel.

I'm not interested in teaching you a method, but I am interested in sharing with you lifeskills that have served me well as I seek to tell others about Jesus. I hope they make sense and encourage you.

Reaching Up to God

It's been said that "we must talk to God about man before we talk to man about God." Check it out: outreach begins with upreach. We need to reach up before we reach out.

From prison, Paul could not be silenced in his Gospel witness.

He wrote, "Pray also for us, that God may open to us a door for the word, to declare the mystery of Christ, on account of which I am in prison—that I may make it clear, which is how I ought to speak."[18]

"Lord, lead me to those You are leading to the cross."

Think of the nonbelievers in your life and consider creating a mental (or actual) prayer list. Begin praying for them and, like Paul, look for that open door of opportunity. My wife once heard someone say, "Lord, lead me to those You are leading to the cross." I like that. God is always on the move, working on people, softening their hearts to varying degrees. So keep talking to God about people and keep your spiritual antenna up.

Equipping Yourself

I previously mentioned ignorance as one of the reasons more Christians don't talk about their faith. The good news is that ignorance can be eliminated from your Christian witness vocabulary. Too often we shy away from witnessing with statements like, "But I don't know what to say? How do I answer their questions?"

Jesus said, "You shall love the Lord your God with all your heart and with all your soul and with all your mind."[19] Defending the faith (apologetics) is the way Christians love the world with their mind. We have to take the time to examine the objections raised against our faith, then intelligently answer them. There really are credible answers to questions like,

- Are miracles possible?
- If God is good, why is there evil?
- Can I trust the Bible?
- Is Jesus really the only way to heaven?

There is no reason why you can't learn to effectively defend your faith. Paul Little writes, "If we are constantly silenced by non-Christians' questions, we are confirming their reason for unbelief."[20]

Evangelism and apologetics are like two wings of an airplane, and the church needs both to fly. Those who evangelize in the twenty-first century realize the great need to be equipped in apologetics. This is God's command and design for us.[21] People will ask curious (sometimes difficult) questions, and because there are credible, convincing answers, we should learn them.

I got into apologetics because I was sharing my faith and getting stumped over and over again. I would take non-Christians' hard questions and treat them like homework. Over time, I felt better equipped to defend my faith. I didn't get into apologetics because I wanted to beat people over the head with the family Bible, but because I wanted to be better equipped to handle nonbelievers' questions.

> Apologetics is a tool that helps us be more effective in reaching people for Christ.

Apologetics is a tool that helps us be more effective in reaching people for Christ. The person who says, "Apologetics isn't important," has just revealed that they haven't been sharing their faith. If you're just beginning to consider apologetics, I encourage you to visit the One Minute Apologist website (oneminuteapologist.com) and watch our online videos. I believe they can really help equip you (also visit bobbycon wayonline.com).

Remember...learn all the apologetics you can, but never forget it is God who saves. You are simply His messenger.

The Master Relater

One reason we lack opportunities to share our faith is that we have little to no meaningful contact with non-Christians. Non-Christians are not hearing our message because they're not within the sound of our voices. The Gospel hasn't lost its power. Christians have simply lost their audience. If we don't know any non-Christians, how can we possibly introduce them to the Savior? The late Joe Aldrich, former president of Multnomah Bible College, said, "Within two years of becoming Christians, most of us lose contact with all of our non-Christian friends." That's a tragedy.

The very best place to begin outreach is with those we already have a relationship with. When we isolate ourselves from unbelievers, we risk falling into what I call "reverse relating." Remember how awkward it was to relate to the church as a new Christian? Boy, I do. But once we start to grow in relationship with other Christians, we can end up with the same connection problem in reverse. Now we struggle relating to the world in the same way we once struggled relating to Christians. Reverse relating. Part of continued Christian growth (both spiritually and socially) is to be able to relate to both Christians and non-Christians without compromising our identity or integrity.

> Part of continued Christian growth is to be able to relate to both Christians and non-Christians.

Jesus Was Aware of Nonbelievers

Without question, the Lord Jesus was the greatest evangelist who ever lived. His example of reaching others gives us an illustration of how we can build relationships with those who need Him. One of the things I notice about Jesus is that He was *aware* of nonbelievers.[22] Let's be honest. Sometimes we're just too busy to notice people. Jesus was always aware of those around Him, looking for opportunities to reveal to them who He was.

The term "lifestyle evangelism" has been used and overused so much in the Christian community that hardly anyone really understands anymore what it means. Jesus clarifies this concept for us. He possessed an attitude of awareness that informed and influenced His actions and relationships.

We need this same kind of conscious attentiveness, a "spiritual antenna" that helps us be more sensitive to those around us. And that's precisely what Jesus was communicating in His final words to His disciples,[23] a passage that is often misunderstood. Some have taken Jesus' words, "Go therefore and make disciples of all nations," to mean that missions and evangelism is something we do "over there...somewhere else." As a result, we call those who travel abroad for the cause of the Gospel "missionaries."

This is unfortunate. The word "Go" here means "*as you are going*, make disciples." This means that being Christ's witness takes place as ordinary disciples go about their everyday lives—going to the bank or grocery store, picking up kids from school, sitting with parents at a soccer game, and so on. *That* is lifestyle evangelism.

> Being Christ's witness takes place as ordinary disciples go about their everyday lives.

I've heard it said, "Don't go to the grocery store to get groceries. Go to the grocery store to be a witness, and while you are there, go ahead and get some groceries. Don't go to the gas station to get gas. Go to be a witness, and while you are there, go ahead and get some gas. And don't go the bank to deposit money. Go to the bank to be a witness, and while you are there, go ahead and deposit some money."

I love that. That is called living aware. And yes, it's a tall order. Jesus meant for His followers to be His witnesses where they are, wherever they find themselves. Dr. Norman Geisler has often said, "You can't be a missionary across the ocean if you're not willing to be one across the street." Jesus made time for people. He was aware.

Jesus Accepted Nonbelievers

Another beautiful thing about Jesus was that He *accepted* people as they are. He didn't say, "Clean up your act first and then we can talk." Think of Levi (Matthew) sitting in his tax booth doing his job. The Jews despised tax collectors in those days because Jewish tax collectors turned on their own people to serve the Romans, overtaxing their Jewish brethren and padding their own pockets. Because of this, they were considered the scum of the earth.

But Jesus reaches out to the scum of the earth. He loves ragamuffins. He's no respecter of persons. He didn't require people to agree with Him before accepting them. We've got that backward in the church. We need to accept people whether they agree with us or not, but not leave them there.

In our culture, people often equate disagreeing with them as being hateful or biased. So we have to work at helping others feel our love and acceptance while not necessarily endorsing their beliefs or lifestyles. We don't need more performance-based relationships. We already have plenty of that in the church.

Our ability to accept people where they are reveals how much our heart is like Christ's. We must stop *labeling* people and start *loving* them. Jesus saw past Matthew's tax collector label. Christ knew that though Matthew's pockets were full, his heart was empty. We have to lose the labels—tattooed, homosexual, black, white, pierced, Democrat, Republican. This must change if we are to be like the One we claim to follow.

> Our ability to accept people where they are reveals how much our heart is like Christ's.

Jesus Initiated Relationships with Nonbelievers

But Jesus goes even beyond this, challenging us to actually *initiate* relationships with nonbelievers and then *invest* time in them. In Matthew's case, Jesus went to his house, where many other filth-of-the-earth "tax collectors and sinners" were partying. And as a result, others took notice, and that's when the trouble began. Don't be surprised when other Christians mock you when you start hanging out with undesirables and outcasts.

> And the scribes of the Pharisees, when they saw that he was eating with sinners and tax collectors, said to his disciples, "Why does he eat with tax collectors and sinners?" And when Jesus heard it, he said to them, "Those who are well have no need of a physician, but those who are sick. I came not to call the righteous, but sinners."[24]

Our Lord was willing to be ridiculed and considered a glutton and drunkard in order to love and accept others. But the Pharisees accepted only those who were like them. Jesus interacted with drunkards, prostitutes, tax collectors, sinners, adulterers, and many other "undesirables."

Jesus interacted with drunkards, prostitutes, adulterers, and many other "undesirables."

I heard of a church that hired a young, hip, ethnic preacher to be one of their teaching pastors. They wanted him to help give the church a new face and help them connect with a younger generation. So this new pastor began hanging out at local music venues and comedy clubs, building relationships with unbelievers in the community. Apparently this was too edgy for the established church leadership, and after a short time, they fired him.

So who would your church consider undesirable? Who is off-limits socially? Who are the "tax collectors" in your community? And if you spent time investing in them and brought them to church, would you be criticized? I'm thankful Jesus is willing to save sinful people...undesirables like you and me.

And how did it turn out for Matthew? He responded to Jesus' call and left his old ways, eventually writing the Gospel of Matthew. From tax collector to Jesus-follower. But it never would have happened if Jesus had ignored him that day in the tax office.

People are in different places spiritually. If we're aware of this, it'll help us pray better and be more in tune when we try and reach them for Christ. But it requires time, love, perseverance, and discernment to build that kind of relationship. It means we have to care enough about them to listen and learn.

- Some people are stubborn, hard-hearted, and far from God.[25]

- Others have an understanding of truth and are closer to receiving the message of the Gospel.[26]

- Some are antagonistic toward the Gospel. They resent Christianity, as Paul did before he was saved.

- Some are self-sufficient, spiritually indifferent, and see no need for Jesus.

- Others are seekers, looking for meaning and aware of their deep need for salvation, like Nicodemus.

- Many are watchers, carefully observing Christians' behavior and relationships.

- Others clearly understand the Gospel, like the Roman centurion who said, "Truly this man was the Son of God!"[27] But they aren't quite ready to surrender their lives to Christ.

- And then some are genuinely ready to receive Christ and follow Him, like the Philippian jailor who asked, "What must I do to be saved?"[28]

So How Do I Tell?

Contrary to a common fear and misconception among Christians, you do not have to preach in order to tell someone about Jesus. That's segmenting your Christianity into "professional versus amateur" status. It also commits the huge error of making witnessing an *activity* that you do rather than an *overflow* of who you are. With all our seminars and conferences, we have created a "second tier" Christianity where it appears that only the highly trained, skilled, and outgoing people can effectively witness for Christ. Jesus never meant for that to happen. Truth is, any person who is in love with Jesus can be a faithful witness. But He wants us to be ourselves and share our faith naturally.

You are the world's greatest expert on you and your story.

One way you can do this is by simply telling your own story. Remember, you are the world's greatest expert on you and your story. Have you ever taken the time to write out your life story? To actually chronicle how Jesus has made a difference in your life? For example, how has He helped you with this list that was once presented to me:

Overcoming guilt?	Regrets?	Loss of loved ones?
Financial difficulties?	The pain of divorce?	Parenting issues?
Foolish mistakes? Self-confidence?	Marriage problems? Temptation?	Relationship struggles? Pride issues?
In-law issues?	Stressful times?	Addictions?
Seasons of depression?	Trouble with law?	Eating disorders?

Most of the time, your life experience is what helps you establish common ground with other people. Paul was great at this.[29]

Your story is important because it points people to Jesus. It shows them how they can trust Him for salvation. Your life tapestry contains good and bad, wins and losses. But woven throughout is the thread of hope and salvation that Jesus gives. Just tell your story.

We often complicate what God intended to be simple. And we dismiss God's power in the simple clarity of the Gospel message. Sometimes we even trivialize basic faith in Christ as shallow, unreliable, or "not enough."

God says, "Simply believe," while we say, "Believe. Give up stuff. Stop doing certain things. Go to church. Join a church. Be baptized. Join a Sunday school class. Give a tithe. And serve in the nursery. Do all these things and we'll consider you saved." We love creating our lists, don't we?

> We often complicate what God intended to be simple.

To believe means "to trust in." To believe in Jesus means to trust in Him and His finished work on the cross to forgive you of your sins, give you a new life, and welcome you to heaven when you die. And this belief produces *a true follower* who does repent, who does give, who does want to be a part of the church. But it all starts with trusting Christ.

Make sense?

Believe. That's it. Isn't that what you did? Isn't that where the change began? It starts with belief. Not some passive cheap belief, but an active bold belief that fully relies on God.

When it comes to being Jesus' witnesses, our lives and mouths work in concert to share the most amazing news the world has ever heard.

God is looking for children who are willing to show the world He is worthy to worship. He is seeking followers who will open their mouths and simply tell what the Lord has done for them.

Will you be that person?

Will you show *and* tell?

GOSPEL APPEALS

- *The Gospel is meant to be more then visualized—it's meant to be verbalized.*
- *Reach up in prayer before you reach out in evangelism.*
- *If we're going to reach people with the Gospel, our love for people must be bigger than our fear of what they think of us.*

Questions for Further Thought and Discussion

1. Do you believe it is unloving for Christians to *not* share their faith with nonbelievers? If so, why are we so paralyzed when it comes to telling others about Jesus?

2. Why must we do more then simply live the Gospel? Why must it leak?

3. What is the biggest obstacle in your life when it comes to sharing your faith?

4. Do you have any nonbelieving friends you can intentionally share the Gospel with?

5. Look up Matthew 28:18-20 and Acts 1:8 and share some observations from these verses with others in your small group.

6. Joe Aldrich once said, "Within two years of becoming Christians, most of us lose contact with all of our non-Christian friends." Why is this the case?

7. Read Luke 10:2 and then spend some time praying together as a group, asking God to use you to reach nonbelievers with the Gospel.

Chapter 11

SUPERNATURAL!

*"O Holy Spirit, descend plentifully into my
heart. Enlighten the dark corners of this neglected
dwelling and scatter there Thy cheerful beams."*

SAINT AUGUSTINE

When it comes to the Holy Spirit, Christians tend to be a
bit polarized, typically falling into two categories. On the
one hand is the *Spirit-phobia* crowd whose motto is: "Preach the
truth and obey God." They're afraid if they talk about the Spirit
too much, people might start dancing or something. And as we all
know, dancing soon leads to card playing and other wild behavior.
These people talk a lot about the Father and the Son, but the Holy
Spirit is treated like a neglected stepchild. They love the truth, but
the truth about the Holy Spirit is often overlooked. Their "trinity"
could be defined as God the Father, God the Son, and the Holy
Bible (not the Holy Spirit).

On the other side of the aisle is the *Spirit-mania* crowd. These
churches and believers typically live from one ecstatic experience to
the next. Some of these experiences involve holy laughter (people
laughing like crazy at one another), an overemphasis of speaking

in tongues, being "slain in the Spirit," or even experiencing convulsions—all attributed to the work of the Holy Spirit. These experiences supposedly prove you've arrived spiritually. Their "trinity" could be defined as God the Holy Spirit, God the Holy Spirit, and God the Holy Spirit. The problem with this group is that many of their experiences cannot be justified with Scripture. But then many of these churches believe God is still giving new revelation (mostly to legitimize their bizarre behavior).

Let's Get Acquainted

The truth is that both these extremes are driven by nonbiblical ideas about God, and neither fully expresses who the Holy Spirit really is. To be fair, both groups have honorable motives—to seek truth and experience God. But typically they "pendulum swing" as they (over)react to the teachings of the other side. Oftentimes, the truth is found somewhere in the middle, between the extremes rather than in the extremes.

I believe the Holy Spirit can and should be experienced, but this experience must always be scripturally grounded. Truth *and* experience. Word *and* power. Education *and* emotion. These are not mutually exclusive. They work together. I believe this confusion concerning the Holy Spirit is causing many in the church to miss out on the supernatural.

Perhaps you've heard so many views on the Holy Spirit that you've just given up on this conundrum and have put Him in the "mystery" category.

Do you know who the Holy Spirit is?

Do you understand the Holy Spirit's function in your life? If someone said to you, "Talk to me about the importance of the Holy Spirit in the believer's life," could you?

Do you know what it means to be "filled with the Spirit" or "baptized by the Spirit"? Are they the same thing, or is there a difference?

Do you know what it means to walk in the Spirit? Are you familiar with the fruit of the Spirit and how it is produced in your life?

Do you know what displeases the Spirit and how to recognize Him when He's at work in and around you?

There are answers to these questions, and you can know them. God wants you to have a biblical understanding of the Holy Spirit so that you can experience His supernatural power. In order for this to happen, we have to be guided by Scripture and refuse to put the Holy Spirit in a box. Not that we can anyway. There is certainly a mysterious side to the Holy Spirit. It's easier for us to grasp the idea of God the Father or God the Son, but the Holy Spirit is a bit of an enigma. Like the child who referred to the Trinity as "The Father, the Son, and the Other One." However, in spite of this mystery, there is much we can know about the third member of the Godhead.

> God wants you to have a biblical understanding of the Holy Spirit so that you can experience His supernatural power.

Who Is the Holy Spirit?

We first hear about the Holy Spirit in the first book of the Bible. In fact, the second verse in Scripture mentions Him. So the truth about the Spirit is not a New Testament thing, but our understanding does crystalize with the additional New Testament revelation. But because there is so much mystery surrounding the Spirit, let's answer some of the most common questions concerning Him.

A Jehovah's Witness will tell you the Holy Spirit is a force or some invisible energy, like *Star Wars* when Yoda tells Luke, "Use the Force." But God's Spirit is not an energy force we tap into through some sort of Eastern, mystical mind trick. Nineteenth-century pastor and evangelist R.A. Torrey wrote,

> It is of the highest importance…that we decide whether the Holy Spirit is a Divine Person worthy to receive our adoration, our faith, our love, and our entire surrender to Himself, or whether it is simply an influence

emanating from God or a power or an illumination that God imparts to us. If the Holy Spirit is a person, and a Divine Person, and we do not know Him as such, then we are robbing a Divine Being of the worship and the faith and the love and the surrender to Himself which are His due.[1]

So if the Holy Spirit is not a force and not an "it," then who is He?

The Holy Spirit Is a Person

When you think of a person, you usually think of a human, don't you? But God is also described as a Person, though not human like us. In that same opening chapter of the Bible, God says we are made in His image. But what does it really mean to be a person? At the very least, a person is someone who possesses mind, will, and emotion. Like God, we have intellect to think and reason with. We have wills, enabling us to make choices. And we have emotions, allowing us to feel (though some Christian philosophers contend that God doesn't feel). Furthermore, we are created as moral beings designed to reflect the ultimate Moral Being—God.

But though we share these characteristics with God, He is a different being altogether. And yet, He designed and created us to share certain things with Him. Theologians call these shared traits "communicable attributes." These attributes help us relate to God on a personal level.

For example, we are like God in that we can be creative, show love to people, make decisions, and have relationships. But we are unlike God in other ways. These are known as "incommunicable attributes" and set Him apart from humanity. Unlike us, God is all-knowing, all-powerful, and perfectly holy. He transcends time. He is eternal. We can't relate on that level. There is no commonality with God on these things.

So having established that, *how do we know the Holy Spirit is a Person?*

One indicator is that when describing the Holy Spirit, the Bible uses *personal pronouns*. Teaching His disciples about the coming Holy Spirit, Jesus said,

> "Nevertheless, I tell you the truth: it is to your advantage that I go away, for if I do not go away, the Helper will not come to you. But if I go, I will send *him* to you. And when *he* comes, *he* will convict the world concerning sin and righteousness and judgment: concerning sin, because they do not believe in me; concerning righteousness, because I go to the Father, and you will see me no longer; concerning judgment, because the ruler of this world is judged.

> "I still have many things to say to you, but you cannot bear them now. When the Spirit of truth comes, *he* will guide you into all the truth, for *he* will not speak on *his* own authority, but whatever *he* hears *he* will speak, and *he* will declare to you the things that are to come. *He* will glorify me, for *he* will take what is mine and declare it to you. All that the Father has is mine; therefore I said that *he* will take what is mine and declare it to you."[2]

Jesus' use of these personal pronouns points to the Spirit's personhood; He is not some impersonal force or energy. Further,

- He is our personal Comforter, or Helper, one called alongside to provide help: "And I will ask the Father, and he will give you another Helper, to be with you forever, even the Spirit of truth."[3]

- He communicates with us: "He who has an ear, let him hear what the Spirit says to the churches."[4]

- He prays on our behalf: "The Spirit himself intercedes for us with groanings too deep for words."[5]

- He leads us: "For all who are led by the Spirit of God are sons of God."[6]

- He teaches us truth: "When the Spirit of truth comes, he will guide you into all the truth."[7] (He is the Spirit of truth, not the Spirit of ecstatic experiences.)

- He raises up leaders in the church: "Pay careful attention to yourselves and to all the flock, in which the Holy Spirit has made you overseers, to care for the church of God, which he obtained with his own blood."[8]

- He can be lied to: "Ananias, why has Satan filled your heart to lie to the Holy Spirit…?"[9]

- He can be blasphemed: "Every sin and blasphemy will be forgiven people, but the blasphemy against the Spirit will not be forgiven."[10]

- He can be grieved and disappointed: "And do not grieve the Holy Spirit of God, by whom you were sealed for the day of redemption."[11]

A mere force cannot speak, pray, teach, lead, be blasphemed, or be grieved. These are all things associated with *personhood*. So we see something much deeper than a force here. We see the Person of the Holy Spirit. But there is another important aspect to the Spirit.

The Holy Spirit Is Fully God

We often associate the miraculous wonders of the Old Testament with God the Father and, of course, the New Testament incarnation of Jesus with God the Son. But the Holy Spirit is often ignored because there is no dedicated record of His person and works.

Or is there?

Actually, we find the work of the Holy Spirit throughout the

Bible. The New Testament writers in particular go to great lengths to demonstrate the deity of the Spirit. Here are a few examples:

- Lying to the Holy Spirit is the same as lying to God: "Ananias, why has Satan filled your heart to lie to the Holy Spirit and to keep back for yourself part of the proceeds of the land? While it remained unsold, did it not remain your own? And after it was sold, was it not at your disposal? Why is it that you have contrived this deed in your heart? You have not lied to man but to God."[12]

- Blasphemy against the Holy Spirit is the worst of all sins against God: "Every sin and blasphemy will be forgiven people, but the blasphemy against the Spirit will not be forgiven."[13]

- He is called the *Holy* Spirit: "The grace of the Lord Jesus Christ and the love of God and the fellowship of the Holy Spirit be with you all."[14]

As Christians we believe in the Trinity. This is a word (though not found in the Bible) that was coined to describe the threefold Personhood of God—Father, Son, and Spirit. This tri-unity means that Father, Son, and Spirit are one in essence and yet three distinct Persons. Many, including Muslims, confuse our belief in the Trinity with tri-theism. A tri-theist believes in three gods, but a Trinitarian believes God is one in essence but three Persons.

Scripture makes no apology when equating the Holy Spirit to the other two members of the Godhead.

Admittedly, this can be a confusing (and frustrating) concept, even for believers. The reason for this is that unlike God's other "communicable attributes" (such as love, forgiveness, will) we have no corresponding parallels of this in humanity. This is a truth about

God that sets Him apart, making Him transcendent or "wholly other." Even so, Scripture makes no apology when equating the Holy Spirit to the other two members of the Godhead.

For example, the Trinity was present at Christ's baptism.

Jesus' command to "make disciples" is followed by instructions to baptize them "in the name of the Father and of the Son and of the Holy Spirit."[15] They are commanded to be baptized in the *one* name and in the *three* persons of the Trinity.

The apostles Paul and Peter also put the Holy Spirit on the same level as the Father and Son.[16]

If you're like most people, you're probably still trying to get your mind around this trinitarian concept. I'd like to illustrate it for you, but we must first realize that *every* illustration falls short and fails to accurately convey this concept. Illustrations can help us understand "three" and "oneness," but they cannot fully express God. Some illustrations actually communicate false doctrine, teaching things that are not true about God. So we must be cautious here.

But to help portray this three and one concept, think of the Trinity as 1 x 1 x 1, which equals 1, versus 1 + 1 + 1, which equals 3. The first communicates three and oneness while the second communicates three separate entities…three gods, which is false. In reality, the Trinity is composed of three Persons, yet one God. Do we totally understand that? Nope. Is that okay? Yep.

> Because He is infinite and eternal, there are many things about God that are beyond our ability to fully comprehend.

Because He is infinite and eternal, by definition there are many things about God that are simply beyond our human ability to fully comprehend. Otherwise, He would cease to be infinite. According to Wayne Grudem, "We may define the doctrine of the Trinity as follows: God eternally exists as three persons, Father, Son and Holy Spirit, and each person is fully God, and there is one God."[17] Confusing? Can be. A contradiction? Not at all.

The Holy Spirit Possesses Divine Attributes

The Holy Spirit is fully God, because He possesses all the same attributes associated with God the Father and God the Son.

He is all-powerful. Theologians call this "omnipotent"—omni = all, potent = powerful.

He is everywhere present (omnipresent).

> Where shall I go from your Spirit?
> Or where shall I flee from your presence?[18]

God's Spirit is everywhere, but that does not mean He is "in" everything, elevating the trees, rocks, and earth to divine status. God is present everywhere, yet separate from His creation. Because the Spirit is in every place also does not mean He *manifests* Himself (or makes Himself known) everywhere. He is both at the bottom of the ocean and present at a church service. Same presence, different manifestations.

He is all-knowing (omniscient). Paul wrote about the Spirit's omniscience in his first letter to the church at Corinth: "These things God has revealed to us through the Spirit. For the Spirit searches everything, even the depths of God. For who knows a person's thoughts except the spirit of that person, which is in him? So also no one comprehends the thoughts of God except the Spirit of God."[19] God has never had an aha moment. He's never felt compelled to get an education. Nor has He thought to Himself, "I'd love to learn more about *that.*" God knows all. Everything.

God has never had an aha moment.

He is holy.[20] Maybe this is obvious, but the Spirit shares the same holiness as the Father and Son. But why "Holy" Spirit? Why not the "Loving Spirit" or the "Merciful Spirit"? Why did God choose to describe Himself this way?

The answer lies in the word itself. For God to be holy doesn't just mean He is "without sin." That is a secondary meaning of the word.

In its root, *holy* signifies being "set apart," meaning God is unlike any other, high above all other created things. It means He is a one-of-a-kind Being. He stands alone. He is God, and there is no other comparable to Him. For the Spirit to be holy says He is transcendent and beyond humankind in all His attributes. It means He is very worthy to be worshipped.

He is the Creator.[21] The Bible helps us to understand that the entire Trinity was involved in creation. Even the word Moses used to describe God (*Elohim*) denotes a plurality, perhaps alluding to the Godhead (or Trinity). He later uses the word *us* in Genesis 1:26 when God expresses His intention to create man. Perhaps the *us* refers to God and the angels or perhaps it's the Godhead dialoguing about the creation of man. Or both. Either way, the Holy Spirit was there at Creation and in the Garden. He made us. He is God.

> The Holy Spirit is the primary Person in the Godhead we relate to daily.

Okay, so now you've been through a Pneumatology 101 crash course.[22] Feel smarter? All that knowledge can make your head spin, but it's important information for every believer, especially since the Holy Spirit is the primary Person in the Godhead we relate to daily.

So what about that relationship? What is the Holy Spirit's role in your daily life, and what does that have to do with being a Fifth-Gospel Christian?

The Holy Spirit Works Within the Hearts of People

Within the Trinity the roles vary between the Father, the Son, and the Holy Spirit. The Father sent the Son into the world, the Son died for the world, and the Spirit confirms this truth in people's hearts. The Trinity is tri-equal, but each Person in the Godhead functions differently. And the Holy Spirit's role is to work within the hearts of people. Here are some of the amazing things He does:

He convicts the world of sin, righteousness, and judgment.[23] Think back on the moment you first sensed your need for Jesus. The time when you were aware of your sin and need for salvation. Jesus says that was the Holy Spirit working in you. This should give us great comfort in our witnessing, knowing that there is *zero* pressure for us to change anyone's heart about Christ. That's the Spirit's job, not ours. If you are a Christian and have ever felt guilt about sin or your lifestyle, it is the Holy Spirit who creates that awareness in you.

He is a vital part of our salvation experience.[24] The Spirit makes *our* spirit alive so we can put our trust in God for salvation. He also washes us clean from sin.

He gives us assurance of salvation.[25] Through the inner witness in our spirit, He gives us the confidence that we belong to God.

> The Spirit gives us the confidence that we belong to God.

He distributes spiritual gifts.[26] Because He made us and knows each of us intimately, He is qualified and able to give us the spiritual gift(s) that will most effectively build up the body of Christ, the church. And He makes sure it's a gift that brings us joy as we exercise it.

He baptizes us into the body of Christ.[27] This is not water baptism, but refers to an instantaneous, mystical, supernatural act by the Spirit at the moment of our salvation. In that instant, He identified us with Jesus, giving us a new nature. We now belong to Him. We are not the same.

He produces spiritual fruit in our lives.[28] As we abide in Him, He develops character qualities in us. It doesn't happen because we merely desire them or will them to happen or even work for them. Rather, He produces them supernaturally over time with growth and maturity. That's why Paul calls it "the fruit of (which comes from) the Spirit." Through this process, we are made into the likeness of Jesus.[29]

He fills and empowers us.[30] There is much confusion among some Christians about the filling of the Holy Spirit. Certain groups would have you think that being filled with the Spirit is *only* evidenced by having an ecstatic experience and speaking in tongues. But that is neither the teaching of the New Testament nor the experience of the early church.

So what did Paul mean when he commanded us "to be filled with the Spirit"? The answer is twofold. The first has to do with the context of Ephesians 5:18 itself and how it begins. Paul urged the Ephesian believers not to "get drunk with wine," which will ruin your life.

Okay, so Paul was an adult. He knew what drunk people were like. And through the inspiration of the Spirit Himself, he thought of this illustration. So think about it. What are the effects of too much alcohol? What does it affect? It influences our:

- speech
- judgment
- physical response
- vision
- emotions

- relationships
- personality
- thought process
- confidence level

In other words, it affects *every part* of us, and usually in a negative and often destructive way.

Paul is drawing for us an important comparison here. He's saying, "Don't be like that." Instead, yield to the Spirit to affect you in the same way being drunk with wine does—*completely*. Paul is saying that when you are "filled with the Spirit," He will influence your speech, judgment, relationships, thoughts, and everything else.

The second key to understanding this filling of the Spirit is the actual word Paul chose. "To fill" is not like the wine filling the glass, but rather speaks of control or influence. So just as wine controls or influences a person, so we should trust the Holy Spirit to do the same in us.

Simply put, this means He's in charge of us. He's influencing all the areas of our lives we previously mentioned. We might rephrase the verse this way: "Instead of being heavily influenced by wine, which leads to ruin, trust the Spirit to influence and control you."

The verb tense here suggests an ongoing filling, meaning it's not a one-time thing but a daily experience. A lifestyle. This fits the concept of a relationship with God. We are not called to merely obey a set of standards or practice a list of moral principles. Instead, we are called to submit to and follow a Person. Paul chose this word because it relates to the Spirit's relational influence in us.

Recipe Versus Relationship

So how are we to apply or experience this "filling" Paul talks about? Is there a five-step process? A formula to follow? A recipe? A verse to recite? A prayer to pray?

Not at all. It's simply a relational choice we make. As you and I go about our day, we merely choose to walk according to the Spirit who resides within us and adjust our lives according to His leading. We consciously rest in Him—His resources and power. And when should we do this? Anytime we sense the need for Him. Anytime we fail. Anytime we need strength, wisdom, perseverance, love, joy, peace. Or for no real reason at all. Just because we want Him to be the One who guides, directs, and influences our heart and mind throughout the day.

One reason this is so important is that it directly affects our witness for Christ as a Fifth-Gospel Christian. As we are controlled and influenced by the Spirit, we rely on His resources, power, and wisdom to tell others to live a life worthy of Him. We draw our answers from the Bible He inspired men to write.

And we depend upon His work in their hearts to change them and draw them to the Son, so that the Father may be glorified.

Being filled with the Spirit will cause us to be concerned about the things He is concerned about, the things close to His heart. And what greatly matters to Him are people's

> Being filled with the Spirit will cause us to experience a greater level of boldness for the Gospel.

souls, the people for whom Jesus died. Being filled with the Spirit will cause us to experience a greater level of boldness for the Gospel, as Peter did at Pentecost.[31] This doesn't mean we'll suddenly stand up and preach before a crowd of thousands. It just means we'll have the courage to speak and be His witness no matter where we find ourselves.

Over one hundred years ago, two young men in Ireland were talking when one said, "The world has yet to see what God can do with a man fully surrendered to Him." The other young man was so moved by that statement, he paused, then boldly proclaimed, "By the Holy Spirit in me, I'll be that man." That young man was Dwight L. Moody, whom God would later use to shake two continents for the Gospel. He was the Billy Graham of the nineteenth century. Moody was committed to being plugged into the Spirit. He was committed to tapping into the power that resided in his heart. Armed with only a fifth-grade education, Moody became a powerful example of a Spirit-filled man.

A woman once chided him, "Mr. Moody, I don't like the way you do evangelism" (referring to his lack of eloquence).

"Well, ma'am, how do you do it?" Moody replied.

"I don't," she said.

"Well, I think God likes the way I do it wrong better than your way of not doing it at all."

Dwight Moody was a Fifth-Gospel Christian. He made a commitment to share the Gospel with at least one person every single day. Chew on that.

Think again of that statement, "The world has yet to see what God can do with a man fully surrendered to Him." It's time for some more D.L. Moodys to say, "I'll be that man. That woman. That boy or that girl." The Holy Spirit loves to show Christ off through fully surrendered believers. Will you be that person? Will you yield? Surrender right where you are? Right now? The world is ready to see the difference the Holy Spirit can make in your life.

Supernatural indeed.

There really are five Gospels, my friend. And though most of your unbelieving friends may never read the first four, you can be certain of this—they're reading you.

God in you is bringing the credibility of Jesus to a watching world. Let's show them how truly awesome He is.

Be a Fifth-Gospel Christian.

God in you is bringing the credibility of Jesus to a watching world.

GOSPEL APPEALS

- *It's impossible to be a Fifth-Gospel Christian apart from the work of the Holy Spirit.*

- *Count on it: the Holy Spirit is all about making much of Jesus through your life.*

- *There are only two ways a person can walk: in the Spirit or in the flesh. There is no other way.*

Questions for Further Thought and Discussion

1. Why do you think there is so much confusion in the church about the Holy Spirit?

2. Look up Galatians 5:16-25 and identify some of the marks of walking by the Spirit.

3. From this same passage, what are some of the telltale signs of walking in the flesh?

4. Do you find yourself seeking the Holy Spirit to produce fruit in your life? If so, what does that look like? If not, why do you think that is the case?

5. Ask yourself, *Do those around me view me as a person who walks in the flesh or in the Spirit?* Get real with each other as a group and share where you need the Holy Spirit to help you grow.

6. Close your time together in prayer, asking the Holy Spirit to help you live like Fifth-Gospel Christians.

ENDNOTES

Introduction: Releasing the Lost Gospel

1. Romans 3:9-18.

Chapter 1: What the World Needs Now Is...?

1. Matthew 9:12.
2. John 3:16.
3. 1 Corinthians 2:2-5; 15:3-4.
4. 1 Corinthians 15:19.
5. Isaiah 14:13-14.
6. Hebrews 4:12.
7. Hebrews 13:8.
8. Malachi 3:6.
9. Ephesians 2:2.
10. Romans 12:2.
11. Genesis 18:25.
12. Psalm 96:10.
13. Psalm 96:13.
14. John 14:6.
15. Matthew 26:39.
16. Luke 22:42-43.
17. John 17:15.

Chapter 2: Image Is Everything

1. John 17:15-17.
2. Genesis 1:26.
3. Philippians 1:6.
4. www.philvaz.com/apologetics/a106.htm.
5. Ephesians 4:1-3.
6. Philippians 2:2.
7. Colossians 3:14.
8. 1 Corinthians 2:2; 15:3-4.
9. Hebrews 1:9.
10. John 2:1-11.
11. Hebrews 12:2.
12. Hebrews 11:25.
13. James 1:2.
14. Matthew 28:19.
15. John 17:15; 2 Corinthians 5:6-10.
16. Matthew 7:1-5.
17. Romans 7:18.
18. Jeremiah 17:9.
19. Ephesians 2:1-3; John 6:44.
20. John 16:7-11.
21. 1 Corinthians 2:14.
22. Ephesians 5:18.
23. Luke 7:47.
24. Luke 7:47.

Chapter 3: Counting the Cost

1. Dietrich Bonhoeffer, *The Cost of Discipleship* (New York: Simon & Schuster, 1959), 89.
2. Luke 9:23.
3. Luke 9:24.
4. Luke 14:28-30.
5. Luke 14:33.

6. Luke 16:19-25.

7. Acts 3:6.

8. Matthew 8:20.

9. Matthew 6:21.

10. Mark 10:17-22.

11. Acts 8.

12. 2 Corinthians 5:17.

13. Matthew 5:10.

14. 2 Corinthians 2:15-16.

15. Thomas à Kempis, *The Imitation of Christ*.

16. Isaiah 55:8.

17. Romans 3:10-12; 8:7; 1 Corinthians 2:14; 2 Corinthians 4:4.

18. Matthew 10:34-38.

19. Philippians 3:10.

20. Matthew 5:11-12.

21. Matthew 5:13-16.

22. Revelation 5:12.

23. John 6:66-69.

Chapter 4: Idol Factories

1. Exodus 32:1.

2. Exodus 32:5-6.

3. Mark Driscoll, "Mark Driscoll on Idolatry in America," October 29, 2009, YouTube video clip, www.youtube.com/watch?v=0rp-QcVEUhU.

4. Friedrich Nietzsche, *Twilight of the Idols*.

5. Exodus 20:3.

6. Justin Taylor, *Between Two Worlds* (blog), "The First Things First Principle," July 28, 2010, http://thegospelcoalition.org/blogs/justintaylor/2010/07/28/the-first-things-first-principle/.

7. Matthew 6:33.

8. Timothy Keller, *The Reason for God* (Boston: Dutton, 2008), 275-76.

9. Alana Semuels, "Television Viewing at All-Time High," *Los Angeles Times*, February 24, 2009, http://articles.latimes.com/2009/feb/24/business/fi-tvwatching24.

204 THE FIFTH GOSPEL

10. www.kff.org/entmedia/entmedia012010nr.cfm.

11. Ecclesiastes 12:8.

12. Ecclesiastes 12:13-14.

13. 2 Corinthians 5:17.

14. C.S. Lewis, *The Weight of Glory*.

15. Psalm 115:5; 135:16; Jeremiah 10:5; Habakkuk 2:18-20.

16. Psalm 42:1 NIV.

17. Colossians 1:15-20; Hebrews 1:3.

Chapter 5: Contagious Joy

1. 1 Peter 3:15.

2. Philippians 4:4.

3. Romans 12:2.

4. Isaiah 42:6-7; 49:6; 60:1-3.

5. Psalm 16:11, emphasis added.

6. While I distinguish between happiness and joy, I equate *ultimate* happiness or *true* happiness with joy. Aquinas appears to use *happiness* in the sense Paul uses the term *joy* or *rejoice*. Therefore, I use the terms interchangeably. Both Paul and Aquinas seek to show that God is the Ultimate Source of joy/happiness. He is the Summum Bonum.

7. I'm thankful for a lecture I heard by Dr. Peter Kreeft, which drew my attention to Aquinas's observations.

8. Hebrews 13:5.

9. Matthew 16:26.

10. Peter Kreeft, *What Would Socrates Do? The History of Moral Thought and Ethics* (A Barnes and Noble Audio Book and Study Guide, 2004), 45.

11. Matthew 20:20-28.

12. Solomon had all the money and pleasure a man could want, but was still unfulfilled. His journal notes are recorded for us in Ecclesiastes.

13. C.S. Lewis, *The Weight of Glory*.

14. Matthew 23:27-28.

15. Romans 3:10-12; 7:18.

16. Thomas Aquinas, *Summa Theologica*.

17. Philippians 1:21.

18. Philippians 4:4.

19. Psalm 144:15 NLT.
20. Acts 16:25-34.
21. John 7:37-39.
22. Jeremiah 15:16.
23. 1 Peter 2:2-3.
24. Hebrews 11:24-26.
25. Psalm 51:12.
26. Isaiah 53:3.
27. Hebrews 1:9.
28. Hebrews 12:2.
29. Psalm 85:6.
30. 1 Corinthians 10:31.
31. Galatians 5:22.

Chapter 6: The Voice of Suffering

1. Nick Vujicic, "About Nick: His Story," *Attitude Is Altitude* (blog), www.attitudeisaltitude.com/about-nick-his-story.
2. "Man with No Arms and Legs Goes on Oprah to Share the Gospel," www.godtube.com/watch/?v=091M0JNU.
3. Romans 6:23.
4. Visit www.oneminuteapologist.com.
5. 1 Peter 3:15.
6. 1 Peter 3:14.
7. 1 Peter 3:15.
8. William Lane Craig, *On Guard* (Colorado Springs, CO: David C. Cook, 2010), 14.
9. John Foxe, *Foxe's Book of Martyrs* (Grand Rapids, MI: Spire Publishing, 2004), 152.
10. James 1:2-4 NIV.
11. Mark 4:35-41.
12. Isaiah 43:1-4.
13. Romans 8:18.
14. Luke 22:41-44.
15. Hebrews 5:7-10.

16. Luke 2:52.

17. Hebrews 12:2.

18. Hebrews 11:6; 10:38; Romans 1:17.

19. Isaiah 55:8-9.

20. Romans 8:28.

21. Romans 8:1.

22. 2 Corinthians 5:21; Romans 5:1.

23. Philippians 1:6.

24. Hebrews 12:7-11.

25. Hebrews 12:3-6.

Chapter 7: Fools for Christ

1. Hayley Tsukayama, "How Many iPhones Has Apple Sold?" *Washington Post*, August 10, 2012, http://articles.washingtonpost.com/2012-08-10/business/35492808_1_galaxy-s-ii-samsung-galaxy-tab-phil-schiller.

2. See Joshua 6.

3. Isaiah 20:2.

4. See Isaiah 20:3.

5. Granted, some scholars contend that Isaiah only had to strip down to his undergarments. Perhaps. Either way, it had the mark of the ridiculous.

6. See 2 Kings 5:1-14.

7. 2 Kings 5:11-12.

8. Judges 7.

9. Judges 7:2.

10. Mark 6:8-9.

11. John 21:6.

12. John 6:1-13.

13. Acts 9:8-18.

14. Isaiah 55:8-9.

15. 2 Corinthians 5:17.

16. Matthew 5:13-14.

17. 1 Corinthians 1:18 NIV, emphasis added.

18. 2 Corinthians 4:4.

19. Ephesians 2:1-3.

20. John 16:7-11.
21. 1 Corinthians 1:21 NIV.
22. To hear Beth tell this story, go to www.youtube.com/watch?v=Xtk5 WgzZcYA.

Chapter 8: Weak Is the New Strong

1. Isaiah 40:29-31 NIV, emphasis added.
2. 2 Corinthians 4:7.
3. David Garland, *The New American Commentary: 2 Corinthians* (Nashville, TN: B&H Publishing Group, 1999), 222. I'm thankful for Garland's insights on this section of Scripture.
4. A phrase not unique to me, but I certainly resonate with it.
5. 2 Corinthians 12:7.
6. 2 Corinthians 12:7-10.
7. Proverbs 6:16-19; 8:13; 16:5; Isaiah 14:13-14; 1 Timothy 3:6.
8. 2 Corinthians 11:24-30.
9. Philippians 1:6.
10. Proverbs 3:5-6.
11. Psalm 119:99.
12. 1 Corinthians 2:16.

Chapter 9: The Ultimate Trump Card

1. Walter Isaacson, *Steve Jobs* (New York: Simon and Schuster, 2011), 596, iPad edition.
2. John 13:35.
3. 1 Corinthians 12:31, my paraphrase.
4. 1 Corinthians 13:1-3.
5. 1 Corinthians 8:1.
6. 1 Corinthians 13:4-8.
7. John 13:34-35 NIV.
8. Galatians 5:14.
9. Francis Schaeffer, *The Mark of the Christian* (Downers Grove, IL: InterVarsity Press, 1970).
10. Robert Robinson, "Come, Thou Fount of Every Blessing."
11. Matthew 5:43-46.

12. I came across these insights about Rembrandt's artwork some time ago, but I do not recall the source.

Chapter 10: Show and Tell

1. Psalm 34:8.

2. Psalm 37:4.

3. C.S. Lewis, *Reflections on the Psalms* (New York: Harcourt, 1958).

4. Acts 4:20 NIV.

5. Glenn T. Stanton, "FactChecker: Misquoting Francis of Assisi," *Gospel Coalition* (blog), July 11, 2012, http://thegospelcoalition.org/blogs/tgc/2012/07/11/factchecker-misquoting-francis-of-assisi/. Also, see Mark Galli's book, *Francis of Assisi and His World* (Downers Grove, IL: IVP Books, 2002).

6. Mark Galli, "*Speak* the Gospel: Use Deeds When Necessary," *Christianity Today*, May 21, 2009, www.christianitytoday.com/ct/2009/mayweb-only/120-42.0.html.

7. Matthew 5:16.

8. Romans 10:14.

9. Acts 1:8.

10. Luke 10:2.

11. Matthew 23:37.

12. Romans 9:1-3.

13. Romans 1:16.

14. 2 Corinthians 5:18-20, emphasis added.

15. Luke 19:10.

16. Matthew 4:19.

17. A quote influenced by D.T. Niles who said, "Evangelism is just one beggar telling another beggar where to find bread."

18. Colossians 4:3-4.

19. Matthew 22:37.

20. Paul E. Little, *How to Give Away Your Faith,* rev. ed. (Downers Grove, IL: InterVarsity Press, 2008), 105.

21. 1 Peter 3:15.

22. Matthew 9:10-13.

23. Matthew 28:18-20.

24. Mark 2:16-17.
25. Isaiah 46:12; Ephesians 2:17.
26. Mark 12:34.
27. Mark 15:39.
28. Acts 16:30.
29. 1 Corinthians 9:22-23.

Chapter 11: Supernatural!

1. R.A. Torrey, *The Person and Work of the Holy Spirit* (Grand Rapids, MI: Zondervan, 1974), 9.
2. John 16:7-15, emphasis added.
3. John 14:16.
4. Revelation 2:7.
5. Romans 8:26.
6. Romans 8:14.
7. John 16:13.
8. Acts 20:28.
9. Acts 5:3-4.
10. Matthew 12:31-32.
11. Ephesians 4:30.
12. Acts 5:3-4,9.
13. Matthew 12:31.
14. 2 Corinthians 13:14.
15. Matthew 28:19.
16. 2 Corinthians 13:14; 1 Peter 1:2.
17. Wayne Grudem, *Systematic Theology: An Introduction to Biblical Doctrine* (Grand Rapids, MI: Zondervan, 1994), 226.
18. Psalm 139:7.
19. 1 Corinthians 2:10-11.
20. 2 Corinthians 13:14.
21. Genesis 1:2.
22. Pneumatology is the study of the Holy Spirit.
23. John 16:8.
24. Ephesians 2:1-10; Titus 3:5.

25. Romans 8:16-17.
26. 1 Corinthians 12:11.
27. 1 Corinthians 12:13.
28. Galatians 5:22-23.
29. Romans 8:29.
30. Ephesians 5:18.
31. Acts 2:4,14.

ABOUT THE AUTHOR

Bobby Conway is lead pastor of Life Fellowship Church near Charlotte, NC. He is a graduate of Dallas Theological Seminary (ThM) and Southern Evangelical Seminary (DMin) and the author of *Hell, Rob Bell, and What Happens When People Die?* Bobby is also the founder and host of the *One-Minute Apologist* (www.oneminuteapologist.com). In addition, he and his wife, Heather, serve on the Family Life "Weekend to Remember" marriage conference speaking team.

To learn more, visit **bobbyconwayonline.com**

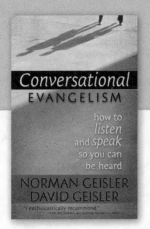

Conversational Evangelism
How to Listen and Speak
So You Can Be Heard
David Geisler and Norman Geisler

Witnessing used to involve laying out the truth and guiding a person to understand and accept it. But the awareness of basic Christian principles has changed and so have the needs of pre-believers. With a passion for people, authors David and Norman Geisler share an engaging, conversational approach to evangelism as they address:

- What makes old models of witnessing ineffective in today's culture

- Why evangelism must start with relational pre-evangelism

- How to ask questions, listen attentively, and understand what someone believes

- Ways to identify the real barriers to belief in order to build a bridge to truth

- How to keep dialogue going with different personality types

This refreshing, practical resource is ideal for churches and individuals. Readers will discover how God uses their everyday encounters for great things when they switch from trying to witness effectively to effectively being a witness through communication and compassion.

**I'm Fine with God...
It's Christians I Can't Stand**
*Getting Past the Religious Garbage
in the Search for Spiritual Truth*
Bruce Bickel and Stan Jantz

Many non-Christians find the behavior of some Christians off-putting rather than inviting. Many Christians do too! Now Bruce Bickel and Stan Jantz, authors of *Knowing the Bible 101*, take an unflinchingly honest and often humorous look at some believers' outlandish behavior. This candid assessment of the church will bridge the communication gap, empowering Christians to share their faith more freely and helping those who don't yet believe discover the truth about God without being distracted by...

- judgmental attitudes, hypocrisy, and condemnation
- confusing mixtures of politics and the gospel
- defensive positions in the "God vs. science" debate
- extreme teachings about prosperity
- unbalanced fixations on the end times
- uninformed opinions about others' beliefs
- unprofessional Christian media and entertainment

This refreshing call to authentic Christianity will help Christians and non-Christians get past the peripheral issues and communicate openly and honestly about God.

To learn more about Harvest House books and
to read sample chapters, visit our website:

www.harvesthousepublishers.com

HARVEST HOUSE PUBLISHERS
EUGENE, OREGON